Revolt Against Heaven

An Enquiry Into Anti-Supernaturalism

by
Kenneth Hamilton

*From God to reality, not from reality
to God, goes the path of theology.*
—Dietrich Bonhoeffer

THE PATERNOSTER PRESS

SBN: 85364 003 3

© Copyright 1965 by Wm. B. Eerdmans Publishing Co.

This British Edition is published by arrangement with
Wm. B. Erdmans Publishing Co.
Grand Rapids, Mich.,,U.S.A.

AUSTRALIA:
Emu Book Agencies Pty., Ltd.,
511, Kent Street, Sydney, N.S.W.

CANADA:
Home Evangel Books Ltd.,
25, Hobson Avenue, Toronto, 16

NEW ZEALAND:
G. W. Moore, Ltd.,
P.O.Box 29012, Greenwood's Corner,
24, Empire Road, Auckland

SOUTH AFRICA:
Oxford University Press,
P.O.Box 1141,
Thibault House, Thibault Square,
Cape Town

Made and printed in Great Britain for
The Paternoster Press
Paternoster House, 3, Mount Radford Crescent
Exeter, Devon, England, by
Cox and Wyman Ltd., Fakenham

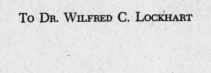

To Dr. Wilfred C. Lockhart

Preface

THIS IS AN ESSAY IN CLARIFICATION. IT IS NOT A guide to modern theology or even a historical survey, although incidentally it attempts to criticize some contemporary theological writings and also to trace some of the lines connecting living theologians with names from the past. Its purpose is to look into the widespread belief that Christian theology ought to detach itself from ideas of the supernatural, and to examine the implications of such a belief. Out of this enquiry come certain definite conclusions concerning the limitations of the anti-supernaturalistic position and the impossibility of combining that position with the historic Christian faith as confessed through the centuries.

The issue is so important that it is certain to be in the forefront of theological discussion for a long time to come. Certain useful books on the subject have already appeared since my essay was undertaken. Among these are Helmut Gollwitzer's *The Existence of God as Confessed by Faith*,[1] Hugo Meynell's *Sense, Nonsense and Christianity*,[2] and E. L. Mascall's *The Secularization of Christianity*.[3] The first of these is written from the position of European Protestantism and the other two from Thomistic standpoints, Roman and Anglican respectively; but I am encouraged to find how much agreement there is concerning anti-supernaturalism in spite of wide differences of theological traditions. If my analysis helps in a small way to clear the

[1] London: S.C.M. Press, 1965 (Philadelphia: Westminster Press).
[2] London & New York: Sheed & Ward, 1964.
[3] London: Darton, Longman & Todd, 1965.

7

ground for further exploration in the area, and if it draws attention to vital questions involving the basis of our faith, the purpose of the book will have been achieved. For one of the characteristics of our time is theological confusion. The trumpet has given forth an uncertain sound, and battle is not engaged. Real cleavages of opinion have always divided Christians in the past, but never has there been so much doubt about where the cleavages actually are as there is today. Yet the Gospel remains God's good news for mankind. The terms of our calling as Christians are still to know the only true God and Jesus Christ whom he has sent. It is here that our thinking about the faith must begin.

KENNETH HAMILTON

United College,
Winnipeg, Manitoba

Contents

9

PART ONE:

Voices Denying Heaven

1

The Theology of Meaningfulness

AFTER WORLD WAR I THE NEW RALLYING-CRY IN theology was "the Word of God." Since World War II it has been "demythologizing." The sequence is all the more interesting because the man who is responsible for the latter slogan is the erstwhile disciple of the man who was responsible for the former one. But Rudolf Bultmann's break-away from the camp of Karl Barth and Barth's high displeasure over Bultmann's present stand have a significance going far beyond personalities. What we see is a complete change in today's theological weather. The winds are blowing out of another quarter and the religious climate is being decisively affected.

If we wish to track the course of the winds, it is good to begin where Barth and Bultmann part company, because the reason for their disagreement is rooted in two conflicting views of theology. The novelty and the offense in Barth's early teaching arose from his insistence that the Christian message could not originate in man but must come to him. The name Theology of Crisis was given to this teaching on account of its emphasis upon the *krisis* or judgment confronting man when he comes

13

face to face with the Gospel. Hence Christian theology was
described in terms of the service of the Word, by which was
meant a faithful imparting of that which has been revealed "once
and for all" (Jude 3) within the community of the Church.[1]
This view of theology was strengthened when New Testament
scholars — notably C. H. Dodd — began to draw attention to the
centrality of the *kerygma* (i.e., the content of the preaching of
the Apostles) in the New Testament record. As a result, the
dogmatic element in Christianity was stressed. The Word was
believed to come to the world bearing its own authority, and
it was not enough for twentieth-century man merely to pick
out some parts of the teaching of Jesus which happened to appeal
particularly to him.

In the Theology of Crisis Bultmann found, if not a home, at
least a congenial resting-place; and, through the twenties and
thirties, his writings echoed its phrases.[2] But in 1941 a new theological concern was voiced unmistakably in his now famous
article *"Neues Testament und Mythologie."* Previously he had
spoken much of the givenness of the Word — God speaks and we
listen.

> The first condition of readiness is this: we must silence all
> other voices; everything we say to ourselves, everything
> other people say to us. For we want to hear what *God* says
> to us. And if we take this seriously there is room for but
> one voice. For God's voice sounds from beyond the world.[3]

Henceforth he was to speak chiefly about the obstacle to hearing
set up by the mythological form of Scripture through which the
Word reaches us. We must first remove the obstacle, and only

---

[1] See, for example, Barth's Gifford Lectures, *The Knowledge of God
and the Service of God* (Naperville, Ill.: Allenson, 1955). The lectures
were delivered in 1937-38.
[2] See, for example, Bultmann's *Jesus and the Word* (New York: Scribner's Sons, 1934).
[3] "How Does God Speak to Us through the Bible?" (1934) in *Existence
and Faith; Shorter Writings of Rudolf Bultmann*, selected, translated and
introduced by Schubert M. Ogden (New York: Meridian Books, p. 167.
Italics in the original. The World Publishing Co., 1960).

then shall we be able to hear what God is saying. At this point, the contrasting views of Barth and Bultmann on the nature of theology appear. Barth believes theology to be a function of the Church. Theology has no authority of its own, but exists in order to prompt the Church to remain faithful to her origins. Theology is a watchman.[4] Bultmann, on the other hand, thinks of theology rather as an obstetrician without whose skilled intervention the Gospel must emerge stillborn. The Word is spoken in vain unless its potential audience has been supplied with the services of an interpreter. Thus he argues that today the real problem

> . . . is the hermeneutic one, i.e. the problem of interpreting the Bible and the teachings of the Church in such a way that they may become understandable as a summons to man.[5]

The earnestness of Bultmann's desire to allow the Gospel to shine forth in its authentic power cannot be doubted. At the same time, he hardly assists us to grasp with precision the full implications of his theological outlook. Why is he so thoroughly convinced that interpretation is the first concern in theology today? Why has a demythologized Bible become such an urgent necessity? He says that the problem is one of interpreting the Bible and the teachings of the Church in order that they may become understandable as a summons to man. But, before we can agree that his presentation of the problem is the correct one, we shall have to look more closely at his basic beliefs about how truths are to "become understandable."

The mere introduction of the technical term "hermeneutics" does not achieve anything. The term simply signifies "interpretation" and is linked traditionally with the principles used by

[4] See his 1934 address "Theology," published as Chapter 3 of *God in Action,* translated by E. G. Homrighausen and Karl J. Ernst (Manhasset, N. Y.: Round Table Press, 1963).

[5] "The Case for Demythologization" in *Myth and Christianity; an Inquiry into the Possibility of Religioin Without Myth,* by Karl Jaspers and Rudolph Bultmann (New York: Noonday Press, 1958), p. 60. The exchange of views recorded in this volume took place in 1953-54.

theologians for interpreting the Bible. By introducing it, however, Bultmann has brought the *question of meaning* into the center of the picture. And the question is obviously a very important one. A meaningless Gospel would be one in which we could take no possible interest. Nevertheless, the question of meaning is hedged about with ambiguities. When we say that something is meaningful (or understandable) we are apparently attributing a quality to that thing, although actually we are indicating how we stand in relation to it. Therefore, before the judgment "This is meaningless!" can be accepted, the query "On what terms?" must be raised. A symphony is meaningless to the tone-deaf, and a board with the word "EXIT" printed on it is meaningless to those unacquainted with the Roman alphabet. Yet both are meaningful to many. Consequently, we are justified in asking Bultmann on what terms he judges that the Bible and the teachings of the Church are not understandable today.

In reply, Bultmann points to the vast difference between the outlook of New Testament times, when the supernatural world was believed to surround and to press in upon the natural world, and the modern outlook conditioned by science. From the scientifically viewed universe the supernatural, the uncanny, the miraculous, and the magical alike have been banished. To men who are strangers to the literature of Jewish apocalypticism and of Gnosticism, the New Testament, which draws from both, is a book of puzzles. Small wonder, then, that the Christian *kerygma,* being expressed in pre-scientific language impregnated with ancient myths, falls on our ears with a totally foreign sound. Those very expressions which once made it readily understood now set up a barrier to communication. Thus it is a missionary concern, Bultmann argues, that informs demythologizing theology. In the thought-forms of our age the identical message once given by a Paul or a John can be recreated for the present-day hearer, who otherwise would remain untouched by Epistle or Gospel.

Such an argument would be easy to accept — indeed impossible to resist — if it limited itself to the intention of eliminating obscurities of language in order to open up communication between the first century and the twentieth. The problem would be seen, in that event, as one of historical understanding and of preserving the continuity of Christian belief in spite of linguistic and cultural changes. However, Bultmann thinks of much more than bridging some historical gaps or entering into a living dialogue with the past. Rather, the past is to be brought into step with the present; for demythologizing means a stripping away of outmoded and unacceptable views of reality. Bultmann takes for granted that modern man not only knows more than his ancestors about the physical constitution of the universe but also has reached a stage in his comprehension of the total nature of the universe where he has nothing of consequence to unlearn. It follows that modern man's conversion to Christianity depends upon an interpretation of the *kerygma* freeing it from the past so completely that it becomes worthy of present consideration.

It is exactly at this point that the terms on which Bultmann judges the Christian *kerygma* to have lost its meaning for present-day man become questionable. Conceivably, modern man's picture of the universe may not be complete in all respects. Conceivably, the Bible may have something to teach him concerning aspects of reality other than those with which the natural sciences deal. It is by no means a foregone conclusion that we have no problems over interpreting the universe until we encounter the Bible and the teachings of the Church, or that these (and these alone) have to be made understandable. Why should we not find in the Bible and the teachings of the Church material which informs our understanding? Why should not the substance of the Christian faith contribute to our vision of what is meaningful? Such questions Bultmann never considers. He looks upon biblical and doctrinal statements as lacking in meaning until they have been fitted into an independent world-view, and he finds what he believes to be an acceptable world-view in the early writings of Martin Heidegger. Here, seemingly, is a

suitable frame of reference for modern man — and thus for a
modern translation of the historic Christian faith. Heidegger
has to speak first, so that God may be heard subsequently.

The adequacy of Bultmann's proposed translation is a matter
for separate investigation.[6] What concerns us at the moment is
the fact that Bultmann turns away from Scripture and the Church
to a secular philosophy when he wishes to find some foundation
for meaning. Although he is a theologian he does not think that
theology is understandable on its own terms. He assumes the
need for some translation or other before the *kerygma* can become
"a summons to man." The basis of his assumption is that the
missionary effort of the Church can be effective only if it approaches contemporary man on his own ground and under conditions acceptable to him. This basis is spelled out in detail by
Schubert M. Ogden, who places himself "left" of Bultmann because he thinks that demythologizing should be carried farther
than Bultmann himself takes it. In *Christ Without Myth* Ogden
writes that we run the risk of forgetting that God needs his
creatures to accomplish his work in the world

> . . . when we assume, as we too often do, that we can con-
> tinue to preach the gospel in a form that makes it seem in-
> credible and irrelevant to cultured men. Until we translate
> this gospel into a language that enlightened men today can
> understand, we are depriving ourselves of the very re-
> sources on which the continued success of our witness
> most certainly depends.[7]

Here the missionary motive is proclaimed as the driving one.
Yet, almost in the same breath, Ogden suggests that the translation of the Gospel into culturally acceptable terms is not merely the condition for our witnessing to others but is essential to
our own response to the Gospel.

[6] See below, Chapter 7.
[7] *Christ Without Myth; A Study Based on the Theology of Rudolf
Bultmann* (New York: Harper & Brothers, 1961), p. 130.

> If to be a Christian means to say yes where I otherwise
> say no, or where I do not have the right to say anything
> at all, then my only choice is to refuse to be a Christian.[8]

Another writer, Paul M. van Buren, says emphatically that faith
must find a new expression for the sake of the insider more than
for the sake of the outsider.

> Our picture, however, is of the Christian, himself a secular
> man, who realizes that the juxtaposition of his faith, ex-
> pressed in traditional terms, and his ordinary way of think-
> ing, causes a spiritual schizophrenia.[9]

Ogden and van Buren agree that there is no future for a Christianity which fails to fall into line with the current interpretation
of the universe.

There is evidence, then, of a movement toward what may be
termed a Theology of Meaningfulness. Instead of stressing the
Word which addresses man, theology at the moment is concentrating upon man's capacity to speak about his own destiny in
his own words. It asks how far the Christian Gospel can be considered credible and relevant to enlightened men today. The
desire to show faith to be credible and relevant is a worthy one,
yet any attempt to reach the stated goal of contemporary meaningfulness must reckon with a twofold difficulty.

The first difficulty is to reach an agreement concerning what,
in fact, is understandable to enlightened men today. It sounds
plausible to argue that the Christian Gospel cannot get home
to modern man unless it is translated into terms meaningful to
him in his cultural situation. But the trouble is that different interpreters of the present-day cultural situation advance conflicting reports. For example, Ogden and van Buren agree that
the traditional terms of Christian preaching are unenlightening.

---

[8] *Ibid.*
[9] *The Secular Meaning of the Gospel, Based on an Analysis of Its
Language* (New York: Macmillan, 1963), p. 77.

They agree on nothing else. With direct reference to Ogden, van Buren states: "One wonders where the left wing existentialist theologians have found their 'modern man.' "[10] Apparently, the translation of the *kerygma* into a language meaningful to our contemporaries must wait upon an investigation into the true nature of contemporaneity. To put the issue in van Buren's terms, the Christian believer must ask himself in all seriousness: "Am I really a modern man?" Or perhaps the question ought to be: "Am I suffering from the right brand of spiritual schizophrenia?"

The second difficulty grows out of (or lies behind) the first. If there is no absolute consensus on the matter of what is meaningful to modern man, that is because there is no universal standard of meaningfulness to which appeal can be made. That which one person may declare to be most meaningful another person may judge to be "full of sound and fury, signifying nothing." Certainly, whenever a claim is made with respect to meaningfulness or meaninglessness, the question "On what terms?" must always be asked. The answer to this question, and nothing less than the answer to this question, permits us to gain insight into the situation. And without such insight, we are in the position of someone who is told over the telephone, "I see nothing." The remark will convey definite information to him only if he knows whether the speaker is permanently blind, temporarily dazzled, has his eyes closed, is sitting in total darkness, or simply sees nothing significant in his line of vision.

We have already touched on the radical ambiguity of the words "meaningful" and "understandable" in connection with Bultmann's argument that the content of Christian preaching must be understandable, noting also that Bultmann does not clarify his argument by referring to the "hermeneutic" problem. What we want to know are the terms upon which he proposes to solve the problem. In fact, he adopts a general theory of

10 *Ibid.*

meaning borrowed from Heidegger as his solution.[11] The consequence is that he interprets the total Christian message in terms of his reading of Heidegger's (non-Christian) philosophy. He assumes that this is *the* philosophy to open up the secret of intelligibility and to lay bare reality. So his plea that the Bible and the teachings of the Church become understandable as a summons to man has to be read in the light of Heidegger's "existentialist" interpretation of the nature of man. According to Heidegger, man has the capacity to pass from inauthentic to authentic existence. Bultmann, consequently, assumes that the Christian message of salvation must be understood as a summons to man to discover authentic existence.

The terms upon which Bultmann claims to have solved the problem of interpretation are relatively clear, because he has adopted a particular philosophy and appeals to it quite openly. However, not every interpreter of the meaning of Christianity for our age presents so direct an answer to the question "On what terms?" Thus van Buren sets out to expound what he calls the "secular" meaning of the Gospel. He begins by suggesting that those who believe in an existentialist philosophy, as Bultmann and Ogden do, are deceiving themselves; for, he argues, existentialism does not provide a world-view acceptable to Western man as he is. Indeed, van Buren is skeptical about the whole idea of searching for any definitive world-view in our day. He thinks that it may be proper to apply the label "secular" to the broad way of looking at the universe which is most common among us, but he points out that the label means different things to different people. He does not claim to have found "a neutral ground" from which to describe "the way things are." The most

---

[11] In his essay "Word of God and Hermeneutics" Gerhard Ebeling comments that hermeneutics, as Bultmann develops it, has become the essence of philosophy, embracing epistemology and ontology. He traces the pedigree of this view from Schleiermacher via Dilthey to Heidegger (*Word and Faith*, Philadelphia: Fortress Press, 1963, pp. 305-32). Ebeling's essay also appears as one of the two "focal essays" in *The New Hermeneutic*, Volume II of *New Frontiers in Theology*, edited by James M. Robinson and John B. Cobb, Jr. (New York: Harper & Row, 1964), pp. 78-110.

that can be said, he urges, is that secularism involves turning
away from the philosophical idealism dominant in the nineteenth century in order to favor an empirical viewpoint.

> To develop an interpretation of the Gospel on the basis of
> certain empirical attitudes, therefore, hardly serves an apol-
> ogetic interest in making the Gospel understandable or
> more available to contemporary "unbelievers." It can only
> serve the purpose of faith seeking understanding.[12]

So van Buren substitutes for the doctrinaire translation of the
Gospel into the language of some philosophy elevated into a
norm with his own more cautious proposal, namely, an interpretation of the Gospel which shall help contemporary empirically
minded believers to understand their faith.

This proposal van Buren makes is an interesting one. It
clearly relates itself to Barth's argument that the Christian should
avail himself of Anselm's theological method, in which faith is
the starting-point and understanding follows.[13] Yet whether it
succeeds in escaping those dangers which lie (as van Buren
sees) in a restatement of the Gospel is far from certain. To
begin with, the mere act of setting up the believer in place of
the unbeliever as the person for whom the Gospel is to be made
understandable does not alter the tendencies inherent in this
theological approach. Whoever is involved, interpretation is
interpretation still; and everything depends upon the nature of
the interpretation proposed. If this interpretation distorts the
Gospel, the purpose of faith seeking understanding will be
thwarted instead of served. A misleading interpretation of the
kerygma is no less harmful for the believer than it is for the unbeliever. Furthermore, one does not banish "an apologetic interest" by explaining that the Gospel is to be interpreted "on
the basis of certain empirical attitudes." Attitudes do not appear

---

[12] *The Secular Meaning of the Gospel,* p. 20.
[13] See Karl Barth's study *Anselm: Fides Quaerens Intellectum* (Richmond: John Knox Press, 1960). Van Buren wrote his doctoral disserta-
tion at Basel under Barth, and he is the translator of a collection of Barth's
addresses, *God Here and Now* (New York: Harper & Row, 1964).

without a cause. They indicate the presence of certain very
definite beliefs, although these beliefs may not be consciously
formulated. They are that part of the iceberg which shows
above water. In point of fact, precisely because van Buren's
secular outlook is not clearly defined it must arouse misgivings.
In spite of his disclaimer, we cannot know for certain that it is
not a hidden laying down of a "neutral ground" to be used to
describe "the way things are." After all, the sole positive information he gives us concerning the nature of the secular outlook
is that it is definitely at ·odds with faith defined in traditional
terms. He asks us, in effect, to accept interpretation on a particular basis without knowing exactly what that basis is. He wishes
to sell us a pig in a sack by assuring us that the sack is made to
a very popular design.

Whether or not translating the Gospel into "secular" terms is
likely to prove more profitable than translating it into "existentialist" terms is another question to be argued in another place.[14]
But what needs no additional argument is the fact that van
Buren's desire to provide the Gospel with a secular meaning is
no different in principle from Bultmann's (and Ogden's) desire
to provide it with an existentialist meaning. The two outlooks,
equally, call upon faith to justify itself by standards set by the
Zeitgeist, although they differ radically in their views of what
the Zeitgeist demands.

It is this common assumption which indicates the dominant
trend in today's religious thinking to be toward a theology of
meaningfulness. That trend can hardly be identified, as van
Buren would like, with faith seeking understanding. A faith
seeking understanding will always be watchful, lest in its search
for what is clear and comprehensible it lose sight of the revealed
"mystery" which is the historic Christian message. The great
creeds and confessions of the Church are reminders of prolonged
struggles in the past to preserve the wholeness of the kerygma
against attempts to make Christianity meaningful at the cost of
ignoring or suppressing those parts of it which did not fit readily

[14] See below, Chapter 9.

into the contemporary world-view. But those who presently advertise their readiness to make the Gospel meaningful by translating it into the language of twentieth-century man never doubt the absolute necessity to exclude from Christian teaching and preaching anything which their favored world-view is not inclined to admit. In this connection, we may glance for a moment at what Ogden and van Buren have to say about translating the word "God" to make it meaningful.

Ogden adopts the view that

> . . . a theology is "mythological," and so untenable, to the extent to which it denies that statements about God may be interpreted as statements about man. By this we mean, *not* that theology may not speak directly about "God and his activity," but simply that whenever it does so speak, its statements must be at least implicitly about man and his possibilities of self-understanding if they are not to be incredible and irrelevant. In *this* sense, "statements about God and his activity" *are* "statements about human existence," and *vice versa.*[15]

For his part, van Buren suggests that even to speak about God is today a waste of breath. We cannot even understand the statement by Nietzsche that "God is dead." "No, the problem now is that the *word* 'God' is dead."[16]

These two differing views display one basic assumption in common. They take for granted that the biblical contrast between "heaven" and "earth" (or between "God" and "man," "spirit" and "flesh") is unbelievable in the present age. We can no longer believe in a realm which is normally inaccessible to us, but which intersects the human realm in sacred story and in the life of faith and worship. In short, all that we have come to call "supernatural" has become hopelessly outmoded; and, if it is impossible for us to believe that reality is twofold — the natural and the supernatural — then it is equally impossible for us to go on repeating phrases that make sense only when nature and

---

15 *Christ Without Myth*, p. 137. Italics in the original.
16 *The Secular Meaning of the Gospel*, p. 103.

supernature are held to be realities with which we have to do. It follows that a translation of traditional doctrine into the thought-forms of a system of truth viable for today is not only desirable but strictly unavoidable. We cannot know what the Gospel is about until we see what it means in terms of the universe to which, as modern men, we are committed.

Ogden is anxious to preserve the word "God," always provided that the word is understood to mean something decidedly not supernatural. He believes that existential philosophy has found a dwelling-place for deity other than heaven, namely man's capacity for self-understanding. Because God in this fashion has a locus on earth, we may talk about him and his activity. Nevertheless, we must never allow our speech to fall back into mythological statements concerning a God who cannot be contained within human existence. In that event, our statements would be incredible and irrelevant to enlightened men. If the divine is not interchangeable with the human it is nothing at all. Van Buren takes the additional step of suggesting that the word "God" has itself become superfluous if there is no specific reality known to us to which it can refer. A supernatural deity is absent from the inventory of evident facts compiled by secular man, so there is little point in retaining a name for a concept without any content.

Taken as winds blowing over the contemporary world, Bultmann and Ogden on the one hand and van Buren on the other represent eddies within one larger flow of air. The prevailing wind may be identified as an anti-supernaturalistic theology of meaningfulness, a theology purporting to give the *true* meaning of traditional religious statements no longer acceptable at their face value. The eddies within the wind arise from different estimates of the "meaning" of religious statements because of different notions held concerning the nature of the world known to modern man. When a secular meaning is advocated, then the bounds of the known world are narrowly drawn to include empirical data alone. When an existential meaning is advocated, then there are wider bounds, since the world of human self-understanding and self-valuation is conceived to be within the circle of the known. But, wherever the bounds are drawn, it is agreed that nothing can exist outside them. So I shall speak henceforth of the Theology of Meaningfulness to indicate the general anti-supernaturalistic position. The Theology of Meaningfulness parts company with traditional Christian theology in repudiating the "Father in Heaven" of the latter. Inasmuch as it argues that to speak about God must be to speak about man and about the world familiar to man (to the point, perhaps, of ceasing to use the word "God"), it has set in motion a *revolt against heaven.*

The terms of this revolt will occupy us in the following chapters.

2

Heaven - and Earth

AS AMERICA HAS ITS SCHUBERT M. OGDEN AND ITS
Paul M. van Buren, so Britain has its John A. T. Robinson.
Bishop Robinson's *Honest To God*[1] is an explicit call for a new
direction in theology, taking the path of meaningfulness.

Robinson begins by speaking of "a growing gulf between the
traditional orthodox supernaturalism in which our Faith has
been framed and the categories which the 'lay' world (for want
of a better term) finds meaningful today."[2] Many thoughtful and
responsible non-Christians, because of this gulf, imagine that
they have rejected the Gospel when "they have in fact largely
been put off by a particular way of thinking about the world
which quite legitimately they find incredible."[3] Here the Anglican bishop sounds the same notes which are heard in Ogden
and van Buren. His starting-point is with the nature of the
world known to modern "secular" man, and with the need to

---

[1] Philadelphia: Westminster Press, 1963.
[2] *Honest to God*, p. 8.
[3] *Ibid.*

make the Christian Gospel meaningful by admitting that anything lying beyond the bounds of the current world-view is incredible. Like van Buren, he believes that a reinterpretation of the *kerygma* is required as much for the Christian as for the sake of the non-Christian. Since he has found "orthodox" teaching to be often remote from his personal spiritual perception, he concludes that the outsider and the insider stand to gain equally from a resolute attempt to translate the Gospel into meaningful language. Like Ogden, he sees the way through for theology in some kind of demythologization. More directly than either of these theologians, however, he turns to the task of getting rid of the supernatural. His chief target of attack is *the God in heaven,* or, as he actually phrases the biblical image, a God "up there."

According to Robinson, we have already demythologized the traditional view of God once; and the time has come for us to do the same thing again, only more thoroughly. A God "up there" is suited to a pre-Copernican "three-decker" universe and is indeed its natural inhabitant. The writers of the New Testament, he contends, took for granted that Christ came down from heaven and, after an interval, returned there by means of an "ascension." It was all quite literal, because it fitted into a coherent pattern of the cosmos as it was then believed to be. But we do not take the biblical language literally today. Our cosmology is post-Copernican, and we know that there is no absolute *up* or *down.* So God is now said to be "out there." No one really believes the "out there" to be actual outer space.

> For in place of a God who is literally or physically "up there" we have accepted, as part of our mental furniture, a God who is spiritually or metaphysically "out there."[4]

To believe in God means ordinarily to believe in the existence of a supreme and separate Being, the God of theism, the God whom atheists deny. But there are signs that the mental picture of a God of this sort is no longer believable and keeps men

[4] *Ibid.,* p. 13. Italics in the original.

away from the Gospel. Perhaps we are being called to leave behind the image of God "out there" as we previously left behind the image of God "up there." And such a step forward may be the means of our discovering what the Gospel really is, through a radical demythologizing of inherited conceptions. We are therefore led to ask the decisive question: "Must Christianity be 'Supranaturalist?'"[5]

The program thus advanced in question form is termed a "reluctant revolution."[6] If Robinson is truly disinclined to overthrow the established order, one can assume that any action he proposes will be urged only after a most careful weighing of the pros and cons. Yet the basis of his revolution is, to say the least, vague. On his own showing, there is no exact correspondence between belief in a God "up there" and belief in a God "out there." The first is literal, whereas the second is spiritual and metaphysical. The first places God within the cosmos. The second asserts that God cannot be so "placed," but has His being independently of the cosmos. It follows that there is no real parallel to be drawn between moving from the first belief to the second and moving from the second to the third. Presumably, then, there must be some special reason for wishing the third to supplant the second. Yet Robinson's principal argument seems to be that certain non-traditional writings on the subject of religious faith have impressed him, while traditional Christian teaching has frequently left him cold. "The inarticulate conviction forms within one that certain things are true or important."[7] In connection with so articulate an author as Robinson, this confession must strike the reader as odd. Surely the conditions making necessary a new spirituality and a new metaphysics ought to be susceptible of more precise definition than that.

The writings which Robinson mentions as having supported his inarticulate conviction are a mixed bunch, and he manages

[5] *Ibid.*, p. 29 (first subheading to Chapter 2).
[6] *Ibid.*, p. 11 (main heading to Chapter 1). Cf. p. 27, "It is for me a reluctant revolution."
[7] *Ibid.*, p. 19.

to suggest that he cannot commend all, or even much, that their authors argue. For instance, he calls as witnesses to testify to the bankruptcy of supernaturalism the following: Ludwig Feuerbach,[8] Julian Huxley, John Macmurray, and John Wren-Lewis. These writers are either non-Christians, or else Christians concerning whose theology Robinson finds it necessary to issue some words of warning. Besides these, he cites three theologians as pointing the way ahead for Christian interpretation, namely, Rudolf Bultmann, Dietrich Bonhoeffer and Paul Tillich. He sets Bultmann aside, because (he says) his program has become so controversial. He finds in Bonhoeffer confirmation of his belief that religious orthodoxy must give way to a "lay" outlook. But he confesses that his chief indebtedness is to Tillich, for it is from him that he takes his expression of the new belief which is to replace belief in a God "out there." A revolution in our understanding of modern Christianity will result if we follow Tillich by ceasing to think of God in the heights and learn to think of him in the depths. This will be a liberating conception, weaning us away from outmoded images of deity.

> What Tillich is meaning by God is the exact opposite of any *deus ex machina*, a supernatural Being to whom one can turn away from the world and who can be relied upon to intervene from without. . . . For the word "God" denotes the ultimate depth of all our being, the creative ground and meaning of all our existence.[9]

The old images of God gave us an idol. The new image will bring us a true realization of transcendence.

----

[8] Feuerbach is the only thinker from another age to be quoted. That may be because this philosopher features prominently in R. Gregor Smith's *The New Man: Christianity and Man's Coming of Age* (New York: Harper & Brothers, 1956), a book which may very well have influenced *Honest to God* to no little extent.

[9] *Honest To God*, p. 47. Note that while Robinson here uses the word "supernatural" he often follows Tillich's preference for the word "*supra*-natural."

> The question of God is the question *whether this depth of being is a reality or an illusion,* not whether *a* Being exists beyond the bright blue sky, or anywhere else.[10]

Together with the atheists we shall be able to turn our backs on the Old Man in the Sky, leaving behind us "the greatest obstacle to an intelligent faith."[11] Belief in God is a matter of "what for you is *ultimate* reality."[12]

The new image of God seems to Robinson to be liberating because it gives us a new frame of reference which is not narrowly religious in character. God is now found in the depth of everyday, non-religious experience. There is no need to turn away from the world to contemplate a supernatural Being. God has become the ultimate significance of the world that is open to all, Christian and non-Christian alike. Yet it is not altogether plain that, having made up our minds about what for us is ultimate reality, we must inevitably have discovered the God of the old and new Israel. Suppose we adopt the faith entailed in believing that the depth of being is a reality and not an illusion. Will this faith be specifically Christian? Or can we be certain, without further examination, that it is a faith even compatible with Christianity? Before assuming anything of the kind we surely ought to look a little more deeply into the depths. After all, we are being called upon to embrace an intelligent faith; and, before we jettison the traditional Christian frame of reference for one which is entirely different, we ought to have a better reason for our decision than a simple desire to stand beside the atheists.

Robinson contends that the new image of God is a genuine break-through in understanding. He says that it is more than a mere change in spatial metaphor, whereas the transition from God "up there" to God "out there" was just that and nothing else.[13] This argument is hard to reconcile with what he has said

[10] *Ibid.,* p. 55. Italics in the original.
[11] *Ibid.,* p. 43.
[12] *Ibid.,* p. 55. Italics in the original.
[13] *Ibid.,* pp. 45f.

earlier. For, if abandoning the New Testament frame of reference was a move from the literal to the spiritual or metaphysical, we cannot refer to that move as a change in directional symbolism. We must recognize it as an *introduction* of symbolism. Then the *change* in symbolism is the one which he, following Tillich, proposes; it is the change from height to depth.

By confusing his own line of reasoning in this way, Robinson has succeeded in drawing attention away from the crucial question raised by his new image of God, namely, whether there is any continuity at all between the God of traditional Christian faith and the God of the depths, apart from the fact that the name "God" is used to describe both. His argument is questionable, anyway, at the point where he contends that in pre-Copernican days God was believed to be literally "up there." We may profitably recall that in the Old Testament the God of Israel is described as the one whom heaven and the heaven of heavens cannot contain (I Kings 8:27). But, most certainly, when God is spoken of as the Father in heaven — whether "up there" or "out there" — he is clearly differentiated from the world and from any aspect of it. A God of the depths, on the other hand, may be identical with some "power" inherent in the world. He (or it) may be the creation itself viewed in some special light, and not the Creator of all.

However, Robinson does not stop to consider any of these things, because, as he sees it, the God of the depths has one overwhelming advantage over a supernatural God: he does not have to be proved. Traditional theology, so Robinson asserts, has been based upon the proofs for the existence of God. This "supranaturalist" theology has started in the wrong place. It has tried to show that a Being beyond the world exists. But, if God is defined as ultimate reality, he is that which cannot be doubted.

> Thus, the fundamental theological question consists not in establishing the "existence" of God as a separate entity

but in pressing through in ultimate concern to what Tillich calls "the ground of our being."[14]

By cutting himself loose from a theology of the supernatural, Robinson believes that he has found a royal road to God. Yet his confidence comes from his failure to consider in an adequate fashion the traditional theology which he criticizes. For traditional theology is not based upon the proofs for the existence of God. It is true that traditional *natural* theology tries to establish arguments for the existence of God, but Christian theology as such builds upon the revelation of God given first to Israel and afterwards to the New Israel, the Christian Church. Just as the Gospel itself is said in Scripture to declare "a way that starts from faith and ends in faith" (Romans 1:17 — New English Bible), so the theology that seeks to explicate the Gospel is set in the context of faith. This is an evident fact if we consider traditional theology in the Reformation tradition, where the one and only foundation of theology has always been taken to be the revealed Word of God as contained in the biblical writings. But it applies also to Roman Catholic theology. St. Thomas Aquinas, who considers natural theology to be a part of theology proper, turns early in his *Summa Theologica* to establish the existence of God. Yet he has previously made it clear that "the knowledge proper to this science [sacred doctrine] comes through revelation, and not through natural reason."[15] The fundamental theological question from the traditionalist viewpoint, then, is not whether the existence of God can be proved but whether the Word of the existing God has been received.

[14] *Ibid.*, p. 29.
[15] *Basic Writings of Saint Thomas Aquinas*, edited by Anton C. Pegis (New York: Random House, 1945), I, 11 (*Summa Theologica*, I, i, 6, ad. 2). Etienne Gilson has explained admirably Aquinas's stand. He writes: "As he himself understands it, theology must be conceived as a science of Revelation. Its source is the word of God. Its basis is faith in the truth of this word. Its "formal" unity, to speak like St. Thomas, depends precisely upon the fact that there is a Revelation, which faith receives as Revelation" (*The Christian Philosophy of St. Thomas Aquinas*, New York: Random House, 1956, p. 10).

Now, a God from whom revelation comes and whose Word may be received in faith must be a Being with his own existence. As the New Testament witnesses, ". . . anyone who comes to God must believe that he exists . . ." (Hebrews 11:6 — New English Bible). It is not enough to appeal to our conception of ultimate reality, because we may have any idea at all (or none) concerning the nature of the universe. Besides, we are a part of reality. Does that mean that we are a part of God? If God is not a Being but the depth of our being, are we, instead of receiving revelation, actually giving revelation to ourselves? It would seem that the denial of the existence of God has left us with the alternative of a godless universe or else a universe in which God must be wholly immanent. Robinson denies this to be the outcome of his denial. Providing a new frame of reference for the Gospel, he explains, is not substituting an immanent for a transcendent Deity but validating the idea of transcendence for modern man.[16] Yet here again he has not listened to the voice of that viewpoint which he considers outmoded, or he would be more alert to obvious objections to his proposals. St. Thomas Aquinas comments that God cannot be simply the "formal being" of everything. "For, if He is the being of all things, He is part of all things, but not over them."[17] St. Thomas makes it clear that, if God is indeed present "innermostly" in all things, this is because he is also "above" creation as an agent acting upon it.[18] Without the "above," God is not God, the Creator, Sustainer, and Lord.

Robinson suggests that we should *press through* to the God of the depths, the ground of our being. But he does not take his own advice. If he did so, he would have to face the question of exactly how we are to think of a God who is in the depths but not "above." He would have to consider the full consequences of changing the directional metaphor from "out there" to "down

---

[16] *Honest To God,* p. 44.
[17] *On the Truth of the Catholic Faith,* trans. Anton Pegis (New York: Image Books, Doubleday, 1955), I, 130 (*Summa contra Gentiles,* I, 26, 8).
[18] *Basic Writings,* pp. 63f. (*Summa Theologica,* I, viii, 1).

here" — which is where the ground of our being must be. He would have to ask what "the meaning of our existence" can be thought to be in the absence of a Creator. And he would have to banish from his theological vocabulary all such words as "love," "trust," "communion," or "encounter," which refer to interpersonal relationships between beings. As it is, instead of carrying his revolution to a consistent conclusion, he falls back on the traditional categories whenever it suits him to do so. Thus he agrees that the only analogy of our unity with the source, sustainer and goal of our life is that of *I* to *Thou*.[19] Yet it is impossible to use this analogy if God is not in some sense *a* Being who enters into a relationship with those whom he has created with an existence of their own. Every imaginable "I" is *an* "I" in encounter with *a* "Thou." The suggestion that we can meet the ground of our being in personal confrontation is plausible only if we endow the word *ground* with the characteristics of a supernatural Being. And then the image of ground (or of depth) becomes completely inappropriate.

In short, Robinson is reluctant to pursue his reluctant revolution through to the end. He repudiates *supranaturalism* with a sweeping gesture, and wishes to keep everything that goes with the supernaturalistic outlook. He says that the revolution is to be brought about by a radical change in our image of God. But afterwards he has second thoughts and confesses that perhaps no one image is wrong and another right.[20] At the same time, he sticks to his belief that Christian doctrine must be detached from dependence upon a supranaturalistic world-view[21] — although surely images must play a part here. He concludes by saying that he does not pray to the ground of his being but to God as Father, adding: "My sole concern and contention is

[19] *Honest To God,* p. 131.

[20] "The Debate Continues" in *The Honest To God Debate; Some Reactions to the Book "Honest To God,"* edited by David L. Edwards, with a new chapter by John A. T. Robinson (Philadelphia: Westminster Press, 1963), p. 235.

[21] *Ibid.,* p. 236.

for the Scriptural revelation of God as dynamic personal love."[22]
Under pressure of criticism of Tillich's doctrine of God, he with-
draws his previous declaration that the question of God is the
question of the reality of the depth of being. He now declares
that the question of God is whether experiences of depth — and
of everything else in life — are to be interpreted in terms of
"Being as gracious."[23] So the question of the existence of God
seems to have turned up again after all, for no one could pretend
that every one experiences Being as gracious. But it comes in a
form that is, to say the least, puzzling. How are we to respond
to a gracious depth of being or a gracious meaning of existence?
And if, as Robinson explains, Being as gracious is equivalent to
the grace of our Lord Jesus Christ, the love of God, and the
fellowship of the Holy Spirit,[24] are we not back in traditional supernaturalism without qualification?

With all these twistings and turnings, it is hardly surprising that
some critics of Robinson should label him an atheist using a
theistic vocabulary, while others should conclude that he has
expounded traditional theology under the mistaken impression
that he is remoulding Christian ideas.[25] Nevertheless, we must
ask why an Anglican bishop, of all people, should become en-
meshed in such confusions. The most likely answer seems to
be that Robinson has been extremely sensitive to the contemporary theological weather, has realized how the winds

[22] *Ibid.*, p. 262.
[23] *Ibid.*, p. 261. Robinson borrows the phrase from John Macquarrie's
Inaugural Lecture at Union Seminary, New York, 24 October 1962. Part
of this lecture is included in *The Honest To God Debate*, pp. 187-93, under
the title "How Is Theology Possible?"
[24] *Ibid.* More than twenty years ago E. L. Mascall pointed out the dangers of defining God as the principle underlying the phenomenal world
instead of facing the Christian confession that God exists. See *He Who Is;
a Study in Traditional Theism* (London & New York: Longmans, Green,
1958 ed.), p. 196 (first edition, 1943).
[25] These two interpretations are to be found in two articles reprinted in
The Honest To God Debate, the first (pp. 215-28) by Alasdair MacIntyre
and the second (pp. 165-80) by Herbert McCabe, O.P. MacIntyre's essay
first appeared in *Encounter*, September 1963, and was abbreviated in the
reprinting. McCabe's review first appeared in *Blackfriars*, July/August 1963.

are blowing, and has decided — without sufficient deliberation — that the Christian Church is compelled to run before the wind and not to set its course into it. He speaks of a reluctant revolution, when all the indications are that he has jumped rather hastily on the bandwagon. The reception given to *Honest To God* proves beyond doubt that he has reproduced very accurately the prevailing patterns of thinking. And the "debate" following the book supports the verdict that he has not done much to analyze these patterns critically. He himself compares the present religious situation with a currency crisis, saying that the Christian task today is a double one: to ask honestly what is the real cash value of the statements we as Christians make, and to find a new currency, one convertible in the modern world.[26] But he is so convinced that we must have a new currency (though he does not know what it will be) that he fails to appraise realistically the cash value of our present currency, and thus intensifies the crisis without bringing it any nearer an end.

The Robinsonian theology promises a revolution, but does not produce a coherent manifesto. At the same time, its very confusions are illuminating. Its attempt to bring heaven down to a dimension of earth shows the strength of the contemporary trend to establish an anti-supernaturalist theology of meaningfulness. And its final falling back upon traditional language indicates that Christian faith cannot simply be detached from a supernatural "frame of reference." There is need, plainly, of a more searching look into the whole situation, both in respect of its immediate historical setting and of its wider implications for the understanding of the Gospel in our generation.

[26] "The Debate Continues," *ibid.*, pp. 243-48.

3

Revolution or Reaction?

ROBINSON'S *HONEST TO GOD* PROCLAIMS THE AD-
vent of a theological revolution. But it regards this as an af-
fair of our generation,[1] and it does not raise the question why
we should be faced with a revolutionary situation just at this
particular moment. It makes no attempt at self-scrutiny in an
historical context. We could not guess from reading it that
theological movements today have a background such as is
indicated by Paul Tillich when he writes:

> More than two centuries of theological work have been
> determined by the apologetic problem. "The Christian
> message and the modern mind" has been the dominating
> theme since the end of classical orthodoxy. The perennial
> question has been: Can the Christian message be adapted
> to the modern mind without losing its essential and unique
> character?[2]

[1] In "The Debate Continues" Robinson introduces his analogy between
the present situation and a currency crisis thus: "The situation could be
described by saying that we live in the midst — or at any rate at the
beginning — of a currency crisis" (*The Honest to God Debate*, p. 243).

[2] *Systematic Theology*, (Chicago: University of Chicago Press, 1951-57-
63), I, 7.

Yet surely this background is very important if we are to judge new developments in perspective. For instance, *Honest to God* was preceded, more than fifty years ago, by *Foundations; a Statement of Christian Belief in terms of Modern Thought: by Seven Oxford Men*.[3] This book was written out of the conviction that traditional theology was being challenged by the contemporary world-view, which was questioning the foundations of "the old beliefs."[4] And it continued an essay on the nature of God arguing that God must be defined as Absolute Reality. This Reality is a rational principle "whose character is the ground of, and is in part revealed in, all finite reality and all actual experience."[5] The terminology here is not identical with that used by Robinson, but it overlaps sufficiently to demonstrate that the underlying assumptions are extremely similar. Two thinkers, divided by half a century, have diagnosed the situation before them and have believed that they have found a solution by changing the traditional image of God.

So we can say, "We have been here before." In both *Foundations* and *Honest to God* there is present the conviction of standing at the parting of the ways and of having to choose between the past and the future, between tradition and experiment. Then, as now, Christianity was declared to be tied to an unsophisticated picture of the *cosmos,* and the suggestion was made that mere theism had had its day. The currency crisis, it seems, has been with us a long time.

What requires an explanation, surely, is why Robinson should assume that the crisis is peculiar to our day; and why he, an Anglican, should ignore the precedent of *Foundations* and turn for help to German theologians. Moberly, Streeter, and Temple (contributors to *Foundations*) are nearer home than Bonhoeffer, Bultmann, and Tillich. The latter, however, are

---

[3] London: Macmillan & Co., 1912.

[4] *Foundations,* Introduction, vii.

[5] *Ibid.,* p. 446. (Chapter 9, "God and the Absolute" by W. H. Moberly.) The writer goes on to contend that his view does not lead to an impersonal God (pp. 454ff.).

post-Barthians; and probably this fact has been decisive, since Barth's theology — though still relatively little read at first hand by Anglo-Saxons — has proved to be a watershed in twentieth-century thought. Barth's influence succeeded in turning the whole theological endeavor of a generation away from apologetics to dogmatics, weaning theologians from their preoccupation with the problem of Christianity and the modern mind, and turning them back to the exposition of traditional Christian doctrine. The result has been that pre-Barthian theology looks old-fashioned today. Even though a reaction was inevitable, sooner or later, it could hardly be acceptable unless it came through those who, at least, had come within the Barthian orbit. And that is how things have turned out. A thoroughgoing apologetical approach, stressing the need for reinterpreting the Gospel to make it meaningful to modern man, is with us again. It has been brought about not by those who have denied the Barthian theological emphasis and derided the whole movement, but by those who, while being impressed by Barth's general aims, have thought him to be "too extreme."

Consequently, when Robinson speaks of the need for a revolution in Christian thinking today, he might equally justly speak of a thoroughgoing reaction to Karl Barth (or to the theological situation which, thanks largely to him, presently exists). He might well link his efforts with the work begun at the beginning of the century, when theologians made significant progress toward re-casting traditional doctrine into terms meaningful to modern man. That Robinson does not take this step is, all the same, quite understandable. Those days seem to lie at the other side of a great gulf, so much has the temper of theological thinking been disturbed by the "neo-orthodox" revolution — which *was* a revolution at its beginnings. Ironically enough, we are most likely to remember how "Christianity and the modern mind" was the leading question then, because of the titles of two books of that era which appeal to us still on account of their foreshadowing Barthianism. James Denney's *The Atone-*

ment and the Modern Mind[6] and P. T. Forsyth's *Positive Preaching and the Modern Mind*[7] were unusual in their age in that they did not agree that the modern mind was the standard by which the Gospel ought to be judged or that traditional doctrine was outmoded. Nevertheless, in spite of the fact that we do not readily cast our glance backward to those days, we cannot avoid doing so if we wish to take an intelligent view of the present. The Theology of Meaningfulness shows itself very clearly to be a continuation, after an interval, of a tradition which most certainly did not begin with *Foundations* but goes back, as Tillich indicates, to the breakdown at the Enlightenment of Protestant orthodoxy. If we consider the writings of Bultmann, van Buren, Robinson, and the rest without considering their historical context, we cut ourselves off from the possibility of understanding them either sympathetically or critically. In that case, we shall find no reason for their agreements and disagreements; for we shall view the contemporary theological weather without sensing any pattern in its fluctuations and without an idea of what is likely to happen next.

Among the theologians of meaningfulness, Ogden is the one who has shown himself to be most alert to the roots of the theological outlook he has adopted. At least, he is the most tradition-conscious (with the exception of Tillich, whom Ogden almost certainly follows at this point). He explains that, if we take Bultmann's call for demythologizing seriously, we have put ourselves on one side of a two-hundred-year-old controversy. We have aligned ourselves with the "liberal" tradition in Protestantism that is associated with the names of Schleiermacher, Ritschl, Herrmann, Harnack, Troeltsch, Schweitzer, and the early Barth, as well as with the American liberals and neo-liberals — Bushnell, Clarke, Rauschenbusch, "the Chicago school," Macintosh, the brothers Niebuhr, and Tillich.[8] In the light of such a roll of names, it seems rather out of place to

[6] London: Hodder and Stoughton, 1903.
[7] London: Hodder and Stoughton, 1907.
[8] *Christ Without Myth*, p. 133.

talk about starting a revolution. The more accurate way of speaking, surely, would be to say that we are eager to pick up again a cause that has never died but is no longer a rallying-point with an immediate appeal. Therefore, to put ourselves on the side of the liberal tradition is most decidedly to come out in reaction against the denigration of liberalism which was from the first, the declared policy of the neo-orthodox movement. Barth, and Brunner after him, sought to overthrow the long dominance of Schleiermacher over Protestant theology. Now that action must be reversed. The hour of the iconoclasts has passed, and the revered icons must be restored to their places.

Ogden's (and Tillich's) historical diagnosis makes sense, linking as it does the present concern to restate the *kerygma* with the mainstream of apologetic theology since the Enlightenment. After all, Schleiermacher began his career by challenging the "cultured despisers" of religion and arguing that Christianity was not to be identified with its orthodox dogmatic shell. Harnack proved to be much more than a brilliant historical theologian when he wrote his *Wesen des Christentums*,[9] arguing that the essence of the Gospel could be detached from the forms in which it has come down to us. And today Tillich tells us that theology should be a rational interpretation of the religious substance of the symbols of faith.[10] There is an evident continuity here both of purpose and of method. Theologies of meaningfulness, then, cannot be revolutionary in the sense that they are initiating a new movement which breaks entirely with the past. On the other hand, it would not be wholly right to label the stand they are making as *reactionary*, simply because they are reacting against the dominant theological mood of our time. Rather, neo-orthodoxy deserves to carry that label, because the movement was launched in reaction to liberal the-

[9] English translation, *What Is Christianity?*, London: Williams and Norgate, 1901 (New York: G. P. Putnam's Sons).
[10] *Systematic Theology*, I, 16.

ology, the instrument of the original highly successful revolution against orthodoxy.

Thus it would seem that there is a real need for looking at the latest developments in the tradition of liberal-apologetic theology in the context of their historical development, tracing thereby the course of this "revolution." In such a context the different varieties of theological innovation today would cease to appear disconcerting, odd, or unprecedented. They would be seen to relate to a common center, even though converging on that center from opposite directions. The present study attempts to operate in this area. It tries to show that theologies of meaningfulness follow a consistent, if variable pattern; since the unifying element in these theologies — that which provides their common center — is their opposition to the supernatural in traditional Christian teaching.

Taken to its logical conclusion, the type of survey I am undertaking here would end by giving a history of theological thought extending over two centuries. However, a narrower field has been chosen, because the subject under investigation is not, after all, a historical period as such: it is a pattern of thought traceable within a historical period. And so, although my enquiry ranges through the past two hundred years, with a glance back to pre-Reformation days, it does not pretend to any sort of comprehensiveness. It is selective, and examines the past specifically in order to illuminate the present. At the same time, being selective does not entail being controlled by prejudice instead of by facts. The pattern which emerges out of my enquiry is one, I believe, required by the historical evidence and not simply imposed on it.

The reasons for the division of the enquiry into the sections which follow should be made clear as the enquiry progresses. Perhaps it may be helpful to indicate at this stage why the second and third parts carry the same main heading — "The Earthbound God" — and different subheadings. The main heading illustrates the basic assumption binding together the various phases and forms of the liberal-apologetic "revolution." Be-

cause a God "out there" is denied, some God "down here"
fills the vacant place. Now Robinson has noted that the
metaphor "out there" has implications which he terms "spiritual
or metaphysical." I have argued that the metaphor of depth
(or "down here") also has far-reaching implications. But, whether
or not these implications are made explicit, some kind of God
"down here" is invoked. This God may fittingly be called the
Earthbound God, since he is by definition not supernatural.
He is tied to the world of our experience and is the object of
our worship only because our experience validates his reality.
Such a God can be given the name of "ultimate reality," or he
can remain nameless; but it is all the same in the end. Being
earthbound, he is not *in himself* the subject of faith. If we believe in him, we do so on the grounds of believing that our experience has certain deep, or otherwise remarkable, qualities.

Some forms of belief in the Earthbound God bring out the
metaphysical implications of this belief. Robinson himself
advances a certain way along this path (as when he asserts
that the question of God is the question whether the depth
of being is a reality or an illusion). But he draws back from
exploring the path to the end. He does not go on to ask by
what standard we are to separate reality from illusion. Moberly
in *Foundations,* however, continues resolutely until he finds a firm
metaphysical base on which he is able to build his conviction
that ultimate reality cannot be ignored; and upon this base he
stands and declares that the Gospel, interpreted in terms of
ultimate reality, is meaningful. He chooses the metaphysical
system of Absolute Idealism, but what matters is that he grounds
his theology philosophically. Similarly, Bultmann today grounds
his theology in philosophical existentialism — a different metaphysical system, but nevertheless an explicitly philosophical
grounding for faith. Since there are varieties of liberal-apologetic
theology, then, which appeal more or less explicitly to the realm
of philosophy, I subtitle my second Part of this enquiry "The
Metaphysical-Mystical Approach." The word "mystical" makes
its appearance here because some theologians wish to avoid

specifying any particular philosophy as the one true basis of faith, urging that immediate experience of the divine is the proper foundation for theology. These theologians, nevertheless, usually turn out to be metaphysicians in disguise. Sooner or later they give their reasons why the faith they commend is meaningful and not meaningless.

Part III carries the subtitle "The Moral-Pragmatic Approach." Theologians of Meaningfulness sometimes say that, since there is no reason for believing in a God "out there" in heaven, so also there is no necessity laid upon us for positing a God "down here" named Ultimate Reality or the Depth of Being. God, in fact, should not be named; for a named deity immediately becomes something apart from our actual experience. The most recent theologian of this kind, and one of the most consistent, is van Buren, who argues that we should throw out the word "God" from our vocabulary. This thinker stands in a line with some of the great moralists of the nineteenth century — one remembers immediately Matthew Arnold and William James — who saw religion as the sole effective force calling into play human potentialities and directing these into the channel of right conduct. A Being called God is for these thinkers not only doubtful (does he exist?) but also quite superfluous. What mankind needs is emotional backing for righteousness; and, in religion stripped of doctrine concerning the supernatural, men possess what they need, namely, morality tinged with emotion and the will to believe in victorious living. Again, there may indeed be hidden behind this program for making religion empirically effective some extremely important metaphysical presuppositions. But such presuppositions are never allowed to emerge, unless perhaps in the form of an anti-metaphysical pragmatism or of an equally anti-metaphysical empiricism. For that reason, I consider the moralist-theologians in a section to themselves. They certainly produce a distinctive and easily recognized Theology of Meaningfulness.

Between them, the metaphysical-mystical and the moral-pragmatic approaches represent the poles of liberal-apologetic thought. But there are shades of opinion not cleaving exclusively to one pole. The first chapter of Part III (chapter 8) examines some of these. And there are individual thinkers — Albrecht Ritschl, for example — who turn up in both Parts II and III.

Part IV rounds out the enquiry by looking briefly at the thought of one modern theologian who resisted the trend toward a Theology of Meaningfulness: Dietrich Bonhoeffer. Attempts to claim Bonhoeffer for the anti-supernaturalistic camp throw a good deal of light upon the assumptions of anti-supernaturalism, and Bonhoeffer's own emphatically expressed theological convictions show that the issue of supernaturalism *versus* anti-supernaturalism is no mere matter of presenting Christianity in contemporary dress but involves the very nature of the Gospel itself.

PART TWO:

The Earthbound God

1: The Metaphysical-Mystical Approach

4

Immanence, Transcendence, and Pre-Reformation Theology

ROBINSON'S CALL FOR A REVOLUTION IN CHRISTIAN thinking begins in dissatisfaction with the state of religious terminology. And, in particular, he says that to validate for modern man the meaning of the term "transcendence" is a crucial point in the revolution.[1] An investigation into anti-supernaturalism may very well begin here.

If *transcendence* is taken in its simplest and most straightforward sense of "the quality of going beyond or being superior to," it will be seen to apply to any idea of God whatsoever. In the most primitive faiths the gods are more powerful than men. And, where one God alone is worshipped, this God has no competitor in heaven either; for he has outpaced all other deities until these have simply dropped out of sight. Thus Yahweh appears to the prophets of Israel as one who is "high and lifted up" (Isaiah 6:1; cf. Ezekiel 1:1), and as one who says: "I am God, and there is none else . . . none like me" (Isaiah 46:9). This is the stage at which, according to Robinson,

---

[1] *Honest To God*, p. 44.

God is understood to be literally "up there." Yet to speak of
a literally spatial understanding of God's relation to the world
is misleading. The language used shows no consciousness of
any division of things into the factual and the metaphorical,
the literal and the figurative. Rather, expression is given to the
mystery of the divine when divinity is encountered by the
worshipper. Through concrete, realistic words the imagination
gives form to the experience of a revelation of religious
transcendence.[2]

However, *transcendence* may be a term employed in the
realm of conceptual thinking as well as in the realm of worship
and living faith. In this case, the simple meaning is transformed in the service of logic to become that which can be pred-
icated of a philosophical Absolute. The special feature of the
term within the metaphysical realm is that it is directly linked
with a particular world-view; and this is what most decisively
distinguishes the transcendence known to faith from transcendence as a concept. Worshippers meet (so they believe)
a transcendent Presence, of whom they know only that he has
stooped from "up there" to make himself near to us "down here."
The exact nature of the heaven from which he has "looked
down" and "spoken," or out of which he has "sent his mes-
senger" is really unimportant. Quite otherwise, metaphysicians
call in a transcendental principle solely when such a principle
is required to fill some well-defined place in their systems —
a particular cosmology has need of it. Therefore Tillich, arguing that pantheism is not the doctrine that God is the All but
the positing of an Absolute in the All, rightly stresses that the
label "pantheistic" should never be used without further definition.

> If God is identified with nature (*deus sive natura*), it is
> not the totality of natural objects which is called God but

---

[2] In an essay, "Religion and Coming of Age," included in *The Honest
To God Debate* (pp. 207-14), Daniel Jenkins has made this point forcibly.
He argues that the biblical account of God includes a warning about the
inadequacy of *all* images.

rather the creative power and unity of nature, the absolute substance which is present in everything. And if God is identified with the absolute of idealistic monism, it is the essential structure of being, the essence of all essences, which is called God.[3]

In other words, the philosophers' "God" is the transcendent within a specified cosmology.

When Robinson writes that Tillich's great contribution to theology is "the reinterpretation of transcendence in a way which preserves its reality while detaching it from the projection of supranaturalism,"[4] he ignores the difference between the biblical and the metaphysical interpretations of transcendence. So he thinks it a valid argument that there is a "loss in transcendence" if we cling to the image of a supernatural God instead of adopting the Tillichian conception of God as the transcendent Ground of Being. And he quotes Tillich's statement that the latter "is more religious, because it is more aware of the unconditional character of the divine, than a theism that bans God into a supernatural realm."[5] Actually, the metaphysical view of transcendence has often led to a God who, unlike the God of the Bible, is infinitely remote from the world. So we have the self-contemplating God of Aristotle, the wholly undefinable One of Plotinus, the Nameless God of John the Scot, and Kant's God who creates the intelligible being of moral agents but not their sensuous being. The Judeo-Christian tradition does not recognize the unconditional character of the divine as such, for the unconditional is an impersonal concept belonging to the language of philosophy. If God is God he is not subject to any other Power — which is what "unconditional" presumably implies — but, if he also is a God who speaks to man, he in some sense conditions himself. It may be a gain in transcendence, abstractly

---

[3] *Systematic Theology,* I, 233.
[4] *Honest To God,* p. 56.
[5] *Ibid.* Robinson quotes from the British edition of *The Protestant Era* (London: Nisbet & Co., 1951), p. 92.

considered, to pass over the divine condescension in favor
of the concept of an unconditioned deity. To call this choice
more religious, however, is to take a great deal for granted
in connection with the kind of religion being spoken of. Such
a religion can hardly be a biblically centered religion. And thus
the reinterpretation of transcendence which substitutes a metaphysical transcendence for transcendence viewed in a biblical
perspective is a dubious gain for theology. Does this indeed
validate the idea of transcendence for modern man? Assuming
that it does, modern man is left with a very inadequate notion
of the God who spoke through the prophets and in his Son.

So far, an analysis of *transcendence,* as it is used when
detached from the supernatural, suggests that the biblical
understanding of deity is impaired, if not totally blocked. But
there is still more to learn from the analysis. Transcendence
as a concept used in discursive thought is of service only within a cosmological system. Therefore, although metaphysical
transcendence may well provide a God whose very nature is
to be the Wholly Unconditioned, such a God is at the same
time an earthbound God, a deity whose reality hangs upon a
metaphysician's reasoning; and, if that reasoning turns out to
be faulty, this God simply disappears.

Here it might be objected that a God "up there" or "out
there" is equally earthbound, since the believer's supernatural
God disappears just as quickly if faith in such a God turns out
to be null and void. Yet, in fact, this is precisely where supernaturalism and anti-supernaturalism divide and operate on different levels. When believers confess their faith in the existence
of God, they do so on the basis of a revelation accepted as
authentic. All that they can do is to form some opinion concerning the authority (or lack of authority) of a given revelation, and
to decide to believe (or not to believe) its content. Where revelation is taken for granted, all will agree that only the fool says in
his heart that there is no God (Psalm 14:1). And where revelation
is considered a dubious notion, the general feeling will be that an
undogmatic agnosticism is a sensible attitude to adopt — unless,

of course, the dogmatism of believers is thought to justify the counter-measure of a thoroughgoing skepticism. Yet, when everything has been said on one side or the other, belief cannot create a non-existent God any more than unbelief can abolish an existent one. Attitudes have no effect upon truth. What happens "down here" does not touch realities "out there." Thus, the God of faith may or may not exist; but in any case he cannot be earthbound. And the immanence of this God in his creation is as much a matter of faith as is his transcendence over it. If we start by accepting the fact of divine self-revelation, we can scarely go on to try to prove that the Creator is actually "down here" as well as "out there." To try to do so would be like walking down the street and wondering whether our legs will ever be strong enough to support our weight, or like calling on the family next door and asking them whether anyone is living in our neighborhood.

The most conspicuous thing about the transcendent God of the metaphysician, on the other hand, is that, however remote from the world he may be said to be, his reality is always deduced from the nature of the world. He is a God who is proved as the result of an argument carried on "down here." The argument establishing his reality may be based on the nature of the world of things (via the cosmological or the teleological argument) or on the nature of the world of intelligibility (via the ontological argument). But, either way, argument does the trick. This God deserves to be called *an available God;* for, like Aladdin's genie, he appears immediately whenever we rub the dialectical lamp.

The point is that we have to rub the lamp, and rub it effectively. This is why apologetic theology, being a theology in search of an available God, must appeal to some definite philosophy for its support. Previously I have suggested that Robinson's failure to "press through" to any clear definition of his God of the depths vitiates his whole argument that the traditional image of God is outmoded.[6] His belief that traditional

---

[6] See above, especially pp. 34-37.

theology begins with proving God is, in fact, applicable only
to his own "revolutionary" theology. If the word "God" means
the ultimate depth of our being, in order to speak about God
we must first prove that the depth of our being *is*. Now Tillich, from whom Robinson has borrowed the concept of depth,
elaborates an ontology within which he describes the "structure
of being" — drawing, as it were, a map of the intelligible
cosmos.[7] But Robinson, while saying that Tillich has shown
how the transcendence and immanence of God can be stated outside the "supranaturalist scheme," adds: "Beyond this I do not
wish to be committed to Tillich's particular ontology."[8] In
other words, he is willing to take fruit from a tree but unwilling
to admit to having had anything to do with that tree, which
seems rather inconsistent. *Being*, apart from an ontology, is
an empty concept; and *the depth of our being*, apart from an
analysis of the structure of being, is confusion confounded.
Similarly, *transcendence* and *immanence*, when parted from
the supernatural, are terms implicitly related to a metaphysical
system. So any one borrowing the terms within this context is
already committed to some such system. Anti-supernaturalism
chooses an earthbound, available God, a God whose character
(to adopt a definition previously quoted) "is the ground of,
and is in part revealed in, all finite reality and all actual
experience."[9]

The anti-supernatural view, in short, requires for its foundation a theology of immanence as distinct from a theology of
revelation received by faith. For in this view revelation of the
divine rises directly out of the *cosmos* which we all encounter.
God is not "out there" but "down here" — yes, actually "*in*
here." Thus faith is not required, since what is essential is
primarily a right reading of the evidence continually available to
us in the world of finite reality as this world manifests its
infinite or "transcendent" ground. The transcendence of the

---

7 *Systematic Theology*, Volume I, Part II, "Being and God."
8 *The Honest to God Debate*, p. 260.
9 W. H. Moberly in *Foundations*, quoted above, p. 39.

ground of our being is simply an inference from data immediately present to our consciousness, and so indubitable. And the
situation can be read from another angle, too. Revelation
is necessarily a self-manifestation of God: God alone can reveal God. Therefore, if we define God as ultimate reality, and
if we are sure that we have good metaphysical reasons for asserting that ultimate reality *is*, then we must assume that our
assurance is derived from the working of the divine in our own
consciousness. Revelation does not come to us, indeed, but is
discovered in us. Our assertion that ultimate reality is no illusion is a "God-given" statement, springing from the immanence
of a deity who speaks within.

I have argued that an earthbound deity, who is available in
philosophical argument, cannot have more validity than the
reasoning which produces him. This principle has important
consequences, the chief of which is the authoritative role
played by metaphysical systems in all theologies of immanence.
For here God is not only the end-product of an argument, he
is also *in* the argument and is its necessary precondition. If the
argument is not sound, the immanent God himself has been
proved a liar. So it follows that those who claim to follow a
"more religious" approach to God than the way of belief in a
supernatural deity must always advance some philosophy as
the final explanation of all things (God included). By means
of this philosophy they proceed to interpret all religious statements following the "supernaturalist scheme." Such is the
course pursued by those anti-supernaturalist thinkers supporting what I have named the Theology of Meaningfulness; for they
believe that religious statements become meaningful only when
they have been translated into terms employed by the philosophy they favor, in this manner being brought into line with
metaphysical truth. Such truth needs no interpretation, since
it springs directly out of our own consciousness and is guaranteed by the divine within us: the immanent God.

Another consequence of the principle of God's being dependent upon reasoning is that we ourselves, when we reason

on the metaphysical level, participate in deity. This is the other side of belief in the authoritative nature of metaphysics. If we are aware of the ground of our being, that same ground (though transcending us infinitely) must also be effective in us. We do not need to go outside of ourselves to be able to declare that Being is a reality and not an illusion. Revelation wells up from our own depths. This belief in man's essential unity with the divine may be described by saying that it posits an *internal relation* to God, whereas belief in a God "out there" posits an *external relation*. When an internal relation is assumed, we think we know God by becoming conscious of our true nature. We do not have to wait for God to address us, since he is already "down here." Instead of requiring faith in a revelation received from "heaven," we realize our unity with God through the inward working of reason, or internal revelation, or awareness of Being, which allows us to grasp the structure of being and construct a metaphysic. Whether this view of divinity deserves to be called *pantheism* is largely a matter of how terms are handled. What is certain is that such a view understands God to be transcendent only in the sense of unconditioned, and that it rejects the supernatural because the latter assumes God to be over the cosmos — the Maker of heaven and earth — and not just discoverable in it, available in the rational element in us.

The distinction for which I have argued between the external relation to God posited by faith and the internal relation posited by metaphysics, with the accompanying diverse understanding of *immanence* and *transcendence,* is well set out by Michael B. Foster in *Mystery and Philosophy,*[10] where he contrasts Greek and biblical theology. Foster's analysis is most useful, because Greek theology furnished the starting-point for the development of so-called "natural theology" within the medieval Church. According to Foster, Greek metaphysics was itself a theology. This theology was essentially "mysti-

---

[10] London. S.C.M. Press (distributed in U.S.A. by Allenson, Naperville, Ill.).

cal" in that it revolved around the idea of the contemplation of the divine as mystery, a mystery revealed to the enlightened thinker as he became aware of the divinity within him. Both Plato and Aristotle spoke of the beginning of philosophy being in the experience of wonder and its end in *theoria*, or a "wondering contemplation of the divine, where mystery was not dispelled but more fully revealed."[11] For the Greeks contemplation was a form of intellectual worship in which the soul remembered its own godhead. "To philosophize was to detach the reason from the senses, thus anticipating the final detachment of the soul from the body at death."[12] It was the body, and not deity, which was external to man's true being. Biblical thinking, on the other hand, contrasts man's soul as well as his body with the Living God. He is totally the creature of his Creator.

It was inevitable that Greek theology should influence the expression given to Christianity as the latter became self-conscious and adopted specific theological forms. From the time of the Apologists onward there was a deliberate effort made to win for Christ the riches of philosophy; and even such a figure as Tertullian, who asked scornfully what Athens had to do with Jerusalem, was instrumental in introducing metaphysical categories into Christian doctrine. Although the history of theology shows that biblical perspectives were indeed remarkably preserved in the new forms within which the *kerygma* was set forth, yet sometimes the presuppositions of the Greek world-view were carried into the doctrinal realm with far-reaching results. One illustration of this process is given, in terms very relevant to the present inquiry, by J. K. S. Reid in his study *Our Life in Christ.*[13] Augustine, Reid reminds us, discerns in the constitution of man three elements (memory, intelligence, and love) reduplicating the trinitarian character of God. In spite of his emphasis upon the grace of God, therefore, Augustine finds in

[11] *Ibid.*, p. 34.
[12] *Ibid.*, p. 35. Foster notes the identity of the Platonic "practise of death" advocated in the *Phaedo* and of the Aristotelian "practise of immortality" described in the *Nicomachean Ethics.*
[13] Philadelphia: Westminster Press, 1963.

man something intrinsic to human nature with which God's grace has to come to terms. He speaks of man's need for grace, yet he speaks with equal assurance of man's native desire for blessedness.

> Basic for his understanding of man and his consequent relation with God is the thought that man has substantial being. The course of his argument is then plain: because man is, he reaches out for God. But here evidently the wheel has gone full cycle: this order of things is almost the exact opposite of what appears in the Bible. St. Augustine says: man is and hence reaches out to God; the Bible says: man is made for God and therefore is. . . . The being of man has been broken off from God, and the mending of the breach is ultimately based upon an element in his own constitution. It is thus that in St. Augustine's teaching the desire and search for the *vita beata* gains such prominence.[14]

Reid notes that Augustine links the Christian's decision for Christ with the philosophers' search for the life of blessedness, believing that the two have the self-same motive.

The above illustration occurs within an extended exposition of two contrasting views of man, the *relational* and the *substantial*. Reid's usage here is parallel to my own contrast between the *external relation* to God and the *internal relation;* for the *external relation* implies a genuine relation allowing man to encounter God his Creator, while the internal relation swallows up relationship within identity and explains the character of this identity by means of a metaphysical analysis of essence or substance. When Reid says that Augustine believes the being of man to have been broken off from God and subsequently restored through an element in man's constitution, he is asserting that the unity of the human and the divine in Augustine's

---

[14] *Op. cit.,* pp. 42, 43. Reid in his exposition makes use of Max Zepf's article, "*Augustinus und das philosophische Selbstbewusstsein der Antike,*" (*Zeitschrift für Religion und Geistesgeschichte,* XI, 2, 1959, pp. 106ff.).

scheme of things has never been broken in any real sense. Men remain within the divine Ground of their being even while seeking to experience their secure rootage with that Ground. Reid observes that the Augustinian view is covered by the Greek formula: "all men desire happiness." He disallows Gilson's argument which maintains that Augustine converts the Greek phrase to biblical use by declaring the instinct for beatitude to be a gift of God. For (he says) this gift still remains a property of man, so that St. Augustine's concept must be judged to be "stubbornly Greek rather than biblical."[15]

Reid's understanding of the unresolved tension between biblical and Greek elements in Augustine's thought about man chimes in with my argument that faith and philosophy believe in different deities, each transcendent and immanent in incompatible ways. This same duality has been expounded at length, in connection with Augustine's teachings about love, by Anders Nygren in his celebrated book, *Agape and Eros*.[16] Nygren writes:

> There is a cleavage running right through Augustine's whole theory of love. . . . The materials for the construction of his theory came from different sources. He had found love in the form of Neoplatonic Eros — the soul's homesickness for its heavenly origin, its bold flight up to the world that is beyond all transcience, where all its yearning and desire reach full satisfaction, where its striving comes to rest for ever. He had also found love in the Christian Commandment of love and in Christ's humilitas. In his view these two became one.[17]

Nygren's point is that Neoplatonism and Christianity only *appeared* to meet in a common idea of love, and that Augustine's attempt to combine the two led to a transposition of the biblical commandment of love into terms of loving one's self in God —

[15] *Ibid.*, pp. 43-44. The references to Gilson are to his *Introduction à l'Etude de St Augustin* (Paris: 1931), pp. 1ff., 139ff.

[16] Eng. trans., London: S.P.C.K., (Philadelphia: Westminster Press), 1953 (one-volume edition).

[17] *Op. cit.*, pp. 555, 559.

the surrender of Agape to a philosophers' "heavenly Eros."[18]
Again, the crux of the matter rests in a choice between an internal or an external relation to God.

Augustine, believing that the Word of God was known to the
Platonists, took into his theology the Platonic object of belief.
Augustine's God — on one side of his complex teaching —
abides in human reason, and the eyes of man's soul have but to
turn inward and to the depths of the self in order to discover
the end and fulfillment of his search for the divine. Following
Plato's doctrine of recollection, the Augustinian doctrine of revelation teaches that God is always known, but not always recognized. That we are so often blind to God's presence is not because we are wholly incapable of seeing or because the light of
divinity does not shine around us. It is weakness of will which
does not allow us to recognize what we see or acknowledge what
we know; and so it comes about that faith is necessary in order
that we may wish to see what is within our vision and that we
may learn anew what we already know. Since the springs of
will are located in the capacity to love, Augustine's view that
the intellect is perverted (or clarified in vision) by the quality
of the will is one repeating the lesson of Plato's *Symposium.*
In that dialogue Socrates alone, because of his moral integrity,
is able to declare the true nature of love and describe its power
to lead us from the poverty of the temporal to the plentitude of
eternity. Just so, the Augustinian self is self-alienated until it
learns to turn away from all desires except the desire for God,
its *summum bonum.* Hence we find the Augustinian understanding of salvation stated in terms of the illumination of the soul, and
here both divine immanence and divine transcendence are conceived metaphysically rather than biblically. God is available

---

[18] Nygren's thesis has been contested in John Burnaby's *Amor Dei*
(London: Hodder & Stoughton, 1938) and in M. C. D'Arcy's *The Mind
and Heart of Love: a Study in Eros and Agape* (London: Faber & Faber,
1945). As Nygren himself says in the author's Preface to the 1953 English
translation, these start from premises different from his. They would also
seem to be subject to the same sort of criticism which Reid brings against
Gilson.

to man from "down here," through the light granted to the soul. He does not speak only out of the heavenly places through his Word.[19] Nevertheless, the biblical message that salvation is always God's gracious act is also heard strongly in Augustine. The philosopher in him never extinguishes the believer.

Augustine's bringing together of biblical faith and Greek theology was determinative of the whole course of Christian theology. Yet its Platonic foundation, which gave it its strength, seemed to later Christian philosopher-theologians to be insufficiently flexible. When St. Thomas Aquinas fully achieved his new synthesis on the basis of Aristotle, he started a debate (which has been going on ever since) as to whether the character of his synthesis was set by its true continuity with, or by its radical departure from, the Augustinian outlook. None could doubt, however, that the synthesis was new; for it proposed its own distinctive understanding of the relation of faith to metaphysics.

This fundamental aspect of Thomistic thought is most usually described by saying that Aquinas separated faith from reason, thus bringing about a recognition of the autonomy of reason and freeing philosophy from dependence upon theology. For instance, David Knowles writes:

> As a follower of Albert who outran his master he accepted human reason as an adequate and self-sufficient instrument for attaining truth within the realm of man's natural experience, and in so doing gave, not only to abstract thought

[19] One of the most interesting passages in Nygren's account of the place of Eros in Augustine's thought is where he points out that for Augustine grace itself (as *infusio caritatis*) is the ladder on which we may mount to the Divine life, so that the love of God becomes something to be fitted into the metaphysical scheme — this love is needed in order that we may achieve beatitude. As a consequence, the Incarnation ceases to be first and last God's gracious act in rescuing lost mankind, for it is seen as the means man requires to permit his spiritual self-assertion and his ascent to the heavenly fatherland. Thus grace and the descent of Christ have as their aim human deification (*op. cit.*, pp. 528-30).

but to all scientific knowledge, rights of citizenship in a Christian world.[20]

Nevertheless, there is another way of reading the evidence, and one which reaches quite a different conclusion. It is possible to argue that the "separation" Aquinas introduced did not free human reason but instead bound it to one particular metaphysic which was essentially theological. What was freed, in fact, was faith; since Aquinas excluded revealed truths from the reach of reason, insisting that there were limits beyond which reason could not pass and that where human capacities ended, God himself instructed us. As another commentator on Aquinas, Gordon Leff, argues:

> He was first and foremost a theologian giving a theological response to non-theological knowledge; he differed from his contemporaries in method, not as a philosopher amongst theologians.[21]

Leff points out that it was impossible in the thirteenth century to admit an independent philosophy without putting the teaching of the Church in jeopardy (a fact illustrated in the case of "the pure philosophers of the arts faculty," the so-called "Averroists") and that Aquinas had no such intention. When the Angelic Doctor accepted human reason, then, he accepted it in the terms of his metaphysic, knowing that reason, *so conceived,* could not contradict faith. Of course, we find that those who support the total world-view of Aquinas maintain that his metaphysic is identical with the true substance of philosophy, that it *is* philosophy if that science is properly understood. But the relevant factor here is that the notion of reason and the scope of reason adopted by Thomists is part of a "package deal," and is not adopted apart from a particular theological viewpoint. What is regarded as rights of citizenship (to use Knowles's phrase)

---

[20] *The Evolution of Medieval Thought* (Baltimore: Helicon Press, 1962), p. 257. See also Gilson, *The Christian Philosophy of St. Thomas Aquinas,* pp. 15-25.

[21] *Medieval Thought; St. Augustine to Ockham* (London: Penguin Books, 1958), p. 212.

within this viewpoint looks altogether like bondage outside it. Reason is given a place and told to stay there.

In this connection it is of more than casual interest to note how very different are the estimates of the arguments of Aquinas made by critics who approach his *Summae* from opposing theological positions. We never fail to find, according to David Knowles, "a justice and lucidity of thought and expression" creating the impression "that a veil has fallen away and that the pure light of reason and reality is streaming into our minds."[22] In contrast with this judgment, Richard Kroner complains of proofs giving no real satisfaction because the principles and premises upon which they rest are taken for granted and not argued. "One moves accordingly on slippery ground; one is dazzled but not convinced."[23] We do not need to read farther in order to know which author will be entirely satisfied with the religious thinking of Aquinas and which will find it wanting. But the really striking difference between the two critical views is that the latter alone draws our attention to the basic presuppositions of Thomism as a whole. Knowles simply takes for granted that philosophy, in "the higher levels of metaphysics," is theological, i.e., that natural reason can rise in its own right to a knowledge of God as the center and cause of "manifold being." Kroner, on the other hand, questions the validity of the Thomistic metaphysic of Being; and so his strictures are more searching than are Knowles's words of untempered praise. Emphasizing as he does the overall world-view within which Aquinas drew his distinctions, Kroner confirms, in fact, the accuracy of Leff's description of the Angelic Doctor as first and foremost a (metaphysical) theologian giving a theological response to non-theological knowledge even when he seems to be speaking as a "pure" philosopher.

To sum up: Thomism carries on the Greek view of an avail-

---

[22] *Op. cit.*, p. 256.
[23] *Speculation and Revelation in the Age of Christian Philosophy* (Philadelphia: Westminster Press, 1959), p. 189.

able God established by an indubitable metaphysic. It finds "down here" in the soul's native endowments a sure revelation of the divine.[24] Through his natural reason man is related internally to God. Yet, because Thomism sets the supernatural above the natural, it is able to do what Augustinianism was not adapted to do successfully, namely, appeal beyond the "down here" to an authoritative revelation coming from "out there." Thus the biblical view is added to the Greek view of the divine, faith joined to metaphysics, and a religious revelation requiring believing acceptance set alongside a revelation in the depths of the self requiring only awareness. And, with the addition, there comes into the picture an extra-metaphysical dimension. Man is now specifically related to God externally, through the divine Word which is addressed to him and which he could never discover for himself. The Greek view is not set aside, but it is subordinated to the authority of Christian revelation — God's descent to man.

In the eyes of the non-Thomist the two-story universe of Aquinas appears a thoroughly artificial construction. St. Thomas has married two incompatible partners, or (to vary the metaphor again) has skillfully sewn together two pieces of cloth, but the gaps at the seams show that he has not succeeded in making them into one garment.[25] The non-Thomist also finds that, insofar as the Thomistic system is unified on the basis of a Platonic-Aristotelian metaphysic of Being, there is a departure from biblical foundations. Moreover, when the believer's role is described in terms of his quest for the beatific vision, then Christian faith has been subordinated to a theology which has

---

[24] "In the notion of being the mind grazes the absolute and learns the first law of what is and is intelligible," —M. C. D'Arcy, St. Thomas Aquinas (Westminster, Maryland: Newman Press, 1953), p. 59. The modern concept of the *meaningful* is a somewhat blurred counterpart of the Thomistic concept of the *intelligible*.

[25] This metaphor of the cloth is used by C. C. J. Webb in his *Studies in the History of Natural Theology* (London: Oxford University Press, 1915), p. 286.

its focus in *theoria,* a theology of intellectual mysticism.[26] However, the present study is not directly concerned with such criticisms. It is the positive achievement of Thomism which is most
relevant, and here we are all its debtors. Even if we dissent from
the Scholastic division of nature and grace, we are bound to make
use of the terminology it has bequeathed to us and speak of the
natural and the *supernatural.* For we cannot abolish history,
and the concept of nature is by now so much a part of our cultural heritage that it would seem artificial and intolerably pe-
dantic to refuse to use the word *supernatural* when referring
to the transcendence of the God who speaks from heaven to
men on earth. The biblical contrasts between *heaven* and *earth,*
and between *spirit* and *flesh,* are still serviceable, of course, and
should guide our thinking. They reflect a realistic, dynamic approach to the confrontation of the human by the divine, which
we neglect at our peril. But, because Thomism asserts a discontinuity in knowledge, because it divides heaven from earth
in declaring that Christianity proclaims uniquely and with absolute authority the Word of the One who is "high over all," —
because of this we can be grateful for its witness. In other words,
it is possible to reject the Greek philosophico-theological element in Thomism which is the root of its belief in natural theology and yet to accept gladly its emphasis upon revelation as a
supernatural gift to be received through faith.

The separation of Greek speculation from biblical faith was
the avowed intention of the Reformation. The Reformers turned
their backs upon the teaching of "the Schoolmen," since it
seemed to them that concern with natural theology (the Eros
whereby the divine in man reaches upward to the absolute)

---

[26] Pierre Rousselot's *The Intellectualism of St. Thomas* (Eng. trans.,
London: Sheed & Ward, 1935) demonstrates how St. Thomas's view of
the intellect leads naturally to the mystical religious vision. In this connection, Kroner is clearly mistaken when he attributes St. Thomas's famous words about his theological works being "so much straw" to "a mood
of melancholy" (*op. cit.,* p. 190). These words witness to the mystical
faith that words and concepts fade into insignificance before the union of
man's spirit with the divine Spirit.

had overlaid the biblical message of faith in the living God. Luther especially saw his mission to be one of restoring belief in the transcendent God who was not to be bound by the imaginations of men.[27] Nevertheless, natural theology found its way back into the Protestant camp and flourished there during the heyday of eighteenth-century rationalism. At the end of the eighteenth century natural theology took in a new form, and in this form was to dominate "progressive" Protestant thinking through the next century and beyond. It no longer called itself natural theology, for it regarded itself as making a clean break with the theological enterprises of the past. It declared its program, nevertheless, to be one utterly opposed to the supernaturalism of orthodoxy, both in its Roman Catholic and Protestant branches. Thus, although it was not natural theology in the traditional usage of that term, it was a genuine theology of immanence which proclaimed an earthbound God by means of a metaphysic, either overt or implied.

To this theology I now turn — and to its High Priest, Friedrich Schleiermacher.

[27] This theme is developed by Philip S. Watson in his illuminating study, *Let God be God. An Interpretation of the Theology of Martin Luther* (London: Epworth Press, 1947). Luther's quarrel with philosophy applied to faith is well documented by B. A. Gerrish's *Grace and Reason. A Study in the Theology of Luther* (London: Clarendon Press, 1962).

5

Schleiermacher and Liberal Protestantism

Schleiermacher helped to create the new epoch in theology. In the conflict between Rationalism and Supernaturalism he lifted the old ground from beneath their feet, and raised issues at once deeper and higher.[1]

It was an error common to the old Supernaturalism and to Rationalism, an error full of serious consequences, the thinking that faith is attained through knowledge, that the speculative reason has to prove the title of faith, and this error Schleiermacher confronted with victorious results.[2]

THESE TWO NINETEENTH-CENTURY COMMENTS — THE first by A. M. Fairbairn of Oxford and the second by I. A. Dorner of Berlin — give us a moderately clear picture of Schleiermacher's reputation from the time of his death until the Barthian revolt against his influence. (And even that revolt, although it challenged the correctness of his teaching, did not question

[1] A. M. Fairbairn, *The Place of Christ in Modern Theology* (2nd ed.; London: Hodder & Stoughton, 1893), p. 224.
[2] I. A. Dorner, *A System of Christian Doctrine* (Eng. trans., revised ed.; Edinburgh: T. & T. Clark, 1897), I, 20.

the importance of it.)[3]   It was counted the great glory of
Schleiermacher that he succeeded in bypassing previous theological debates, leaving the debaters standing. And the measure
of his triumph was that he did not found a school but supplied
the incentive for many opposing schools; for those who came
after him, instead of challenging his assumptions, tried to "correct" his conclusions so as to establish with certainty what they
believed he had left imperfectly proven. Those who seemed
to be saying most loudly, "No!" to his thought were actually
doing no more than protesting, "Yes, but. . . ."

When Schleiermacher came offering new theological lamps
for old, his offer was accepted because, after the intervention
of Kant on the philosophical field, natural theology seemed to
be no longer a living option. First in his *Reden*[4] and then in his
Glaubenslehre[5] Schleiermacher introduced religion as an "empirical" reality, beyond the arguments both of the believers who
supported a two-story universe of the natural and the supernatural and of the unbelievers who denied the supernatural in
the name of the (rationally established) natural world. By thus
shifting the area of discussion, of course, he did not alter the
fundamental nature of the discussion. Faith established on
rational grounds was still the desired end. He simply moved from
one type of apologetic to another. The reason which he admitted was no longer the reason of the rationalists or of the orthodox supernaturalists. The reality to which he appealed was
wider and less rigid than theirs. But he ventured into the field
of defining reality, staking everything upon his venture. If we
look either at his methodology or at the content of his theology,

[3] Among many other expressions of admiration, Barth has written: "The
first place in a history of the theology of the most recent times belongs and
will always belong to Schleiermacher, and he has no rival." *Protestant
Thought from Rousseau to Ritschl* (New York: Harper & Brothers, 1959),
p. 306.

[4] Eng. trans.: *On Religion: Speeches to Its Cultured Despisers*, trans.
John Oman (New York: Harper & Brothers, 1958).

[5] Eng. trans.: *The Christian Faith*, trans. H. R. Mackintosh and J. S.
Stewart (Edinburgh: T. & T. Clark, 1928).

we can hardly escape one conclusion. In the last resort, he depends upon an indubitable metaphysic.

It must be granted that his classification of "piety" as a form of feeling opened the way for a great deal of misunderstanding. For many it seemed that a metaphysical grounding was exactly what his teaching lacked. So the Mediating School (of which Dorner was a leading light) argued that his insights needed to be rendered "scientific" by support from some principle embodying cognition. Not only that, but it soon became a stock critical response to label him "too subjective." We still hear it said that religion cannot be rooted in *feeling* and nothing else, since it obviously involves *knowing* and *willing* too.[6] Yet even a superficial reading of the Introduction to *The Christian Faith* shows that, whatever objections can be brought against this central principle of his theology, it was one he had selected with his eyes open. He knew that it would be criticized as one-sided and inadequate, but for him it alone was comprehensive and complete. It was the single avenue to the truth about man, God and the universe. Those critics who come with a "Yes, but . . ." will always have to ask themselves whether their proposals to supplement his principle by introducing other elements from outside do not make his whole position less tenable and substitute the weakness of eclecticism for the strength of a unitary view.

For — make no mistake about this — Schleiermacher's theology of feeling advanced a definite, substantial view of man. Fairbairn, in an admirable summary of the case, allows us to see what was involved.

> He took his stand on religion, and saved it from friends and enemies alike. He resolved it into a thing essentially

[6] "Nevertheless, Schleiermacher's interpretation of Christianity also manifests grave inadequacies and positive faults. In its exclusive emphasis on feeling it is as onesided as the rationalism and moralism which it opposed. Instead of conceiving religion as a response of the whole personality to the impact of God's grace, Schleiermacher singled out one of the 'faculties' as the sole active part of man in the religious experience." —Matthew Spinka, *Christian Thought from Erasmus to Berdyaev* (Englewood Cliffs, N. J.: Prentice Hall, 1962), p. 112.

human, necessary to man. . . . It was the immediate consciousness of the being of everything finite in the Infinite
and through the Infinite . . . it was to feel amid all becoming and change, amid all action and suffering, our very
life only as it was in and through God. . . . But the feeling,
as it was of dependence, could not live in isolation; the
universe was in ceaseless activity, revealing itself to us
and in us every moment; and to be moved by what we thus
experienced and felt, not as separate units, but as parts of
a whole, conditioned and supplemented by all the rest,
was religion.[7]

Religion was *a thing essentially human, necessary to man.* The
essence of man was thus discovered in his capacity for feeling, in
his immediate consciousness of absolute dependence upon the
divine. By going back behind natural theology (with its cor-
relative of the supernatural) Schleiermacher took up again the
Greek theological understanding of the internal relation to
divinity. The being of humanity was grounded in, and inseparable from, the Being of divinity; and to descend into the depths
of our being, to discover beneath the surface phenomena of
knowledge and action the original capacity for feeling, was to
unveil the truth about ourselves and the universe around us.
I have pointed out that a metaphysical theology naturally leads
to describing some cosmology in which the structure of Being
is set forth. And this aspect of things is apparent in Schleiermacher's system also. It was impossible for him to think of man
in isolation from the cosmos of which he was a part. He thought
of religion, therefore, as no accident in the universe, appearing
merely with man who happened to have the faculties of knowing, willing, and feeling. Rather, man through feeling had consciousness of that which made the sum of things into a true
cosmos, a *universe.* In us and through us pulsated the life of
the whole. In our being Being was manifest.

Because Schleiermacher opposed the rationalism of his day,
that narrow rationalism which in orthodox believers and in un-

---

[7] *Op. cit.,* pp. 224-25.

believers alike took *reason* to mean primarily *reasoning*, he was credited with having restored the Reformation faith in a living God. So Dorner wrote: "Now faith, in the pure Reformation sense of the word, has been again reinstated in its post of honour by Schleiermacher, and Christian experience has been recognized as the indispensable preliminary to all dogmatic statements. . . ."[8] And, in our own day, it has been urged that Schleiermacher was instrumental in recovering the "relational" theology of the Reformers.[9] But all arguments along these lines overlook entirely the all-important fact that for the Reformers faith never stood alone: it was always faith in the revealed Word. This supernatural reference was altogether lacking in the theology of feeling, and it follows that *faith* was given a meaning having no connection with the *fiducia* of Reformation theology, which assumed the believer's trust to be trust in the scriptural promises and acts of a transcendent God. Faith, in Schleiermacher's usage, was made "meaningful" by being given an explanation within the terms of his theology, becoming "one of the varieties" of the feeling of absolute dependence. Such an interpretation of faith followed quite logically from a position which assumed humanity and divinity to be related internally (i.e., not in a genuine relation of encounter but as distinctions within a unity). It was true to say, of course, that both the theology of feeling and Reformation theology stressed experience; only the experience was a totally different one in each instance. The Reformers believed in the experience — the fully personal experience — of being addressed by God in the Holy Spirit, who, creating faith in us, enabled us to hear and to respond. Schleiermacher believed otherwise. He believed in the experience of the coming to consciousness in us of that awareness of the divine which was eternally part of our general humanity. What gave

---

8 *Op. cit.*, p. 20.

9 See, for example, an article by Van A. Harvey, "A Word in Defense of Schleiermacher's Theological Method," in the *Journal of Religion*, Vol. XLII, No. 3., July 1962. The other side of the argument is presented in my article, "Schleiermacher and Relational Theology," *ibid.*, Vol. XLIV, No. 1, January 1964.

value to this experience was that it was essentially trans-personal and supra-personal, not being bound to the individual at all.

Certainly, the continuity of Schleiermacher's teaching with Greek metaphysical theology was very patent when he turned to explain what he meant by "being in relation to God." Being in relation to God was the same thing as having consciousness of absolute dependence. That consciousness did not start from a belief in God and a conviction following that we were dependent upon him. On the contrary, the self-consciousness was the prime datum. On the basis of the datum we came to a twofold belief: on the one hand that the feeling must have come from somewhere, and on the other that it must have come to something. And thus we arrived at the notions of God and of human nature.

Here we have all the marks of the earthbound God. To begin with, God is entirely that which we discover "down here" and produce as our discovery.

> As regards the identification of absolute dependence with "relation to God" in our position: this is to be understood in the sense that the *Whence* of our receptive and active existence, as implied in this self-consciousness, is to be designated by the word "God," and that this is for us the really original signification of that word.[10]

Further, the God who appears as the consequence of our perceptiveness is also "transcendent" in being the wholly unconditioned limit of our experience.

> . . . this *Whence* is not the world, in the sense of the totality of temporal existence, and still less is it any single part of the world.[11]

For we are never more than relatively dependent upon the universe around us, so that the feeling of absolute dependence must have its source in the unconditional, the more-than-relative. Finally, the God who is the unconditioned limit of our experience is not to be found other than in and with our experience. He is

10 *The Christian Faith*, p. 16 (§4.4).
11 *Ibid.* (§4.4).

not transcendent in being "high over all" and speaking from "out there" in a revelation which we receive in faith.

> . . . if we speak of an original revelation of God to man or in man, the meaning will always be just this, that, along with the absolute dependence which characterizes not only man but all temporal existence, there is given to man also the immediate self-consciousness of it, which becomes a consciousness of God.[12]

In other words, man provides his own revelation. The divine is known in the human to the extent to which the human can manifest the divine under the limitations of temporal existence. There is "an original and innate tendency of the human soul" to realize and actualize awareness of the divine, a tendency which "strives from the very beginning to break through into consciousness."[13] The divine struggles within the temporal universe, and in man declares itself.

If Schleiermacher's theology is seen to be a theology of the earthbound God and is viewed in the perspective of Greek theology, many of its preplexing features cease to puzzle us. For example, there is his insistence upon the manner in which self-consciousness, when it becomes a consciousness of God, takes us beyond "sensible" self-consciousness and becomes "not the consciousness of ourselves as individuals of a particular description, but simply of ourselves as individual finite existence in general."[14] The reason for this insistence appears when we remember that the earthbound God is always related to some special cosmology. Schleiermacher's God is immanent in the world, but, at the same time, the world *as we know it through the senses* obscures him. We are back in the "two world" system of the Greeks and in what Foster calls the "side-by-sideness" of the divine and the non-divine in nature. So Schleiermacher calls us to battle against sensible self-consciousness in order to arrive at consciousness of God — to forsake the seeming world for the true. When

[12] *Ibid.*, pp. 17f. (§4.4).
[13] *Ibid.*, p. 22 (§5.3).
[14] *Ibid.*, p. 19 (§5.1).

we reach the highest self-consciousness, "we do not set ourselves against any other individual being, but, on the contrary, all antithesis between one individual and another is in this case done away."[15]

> For to the man who once recognizes what piety is, and appropriates it as a requirement of his being, every moment of a merely sensible self-consciousness is a defective and imperfect state.[16]

Thus men learn that as existing individuals they have no true being; for they have fallen away from the divine. But, because they participate in human nature, they are able to touch true being behind seeming being, restoring themselves to their divine heritage. Finite existence in general transcends the merely sensible and is grounded in the infinite and the eternal.[17] Conversely, we can be sure that piety is "an essential element of human nature."[18] Finite existence in general — not the separate individual — has awareness of its status in the real world, the world of the immanent God. Humanity knows its own divinity perfectly, even though an individual may fail to recognize what piety is and thus fail to actualize the fully human state of being.

But, while a comparison with Greek theology throws into relief the shape of Schleiermacher's world-view, the most revealing aspect of this comparison is the light it sheds upon his basic concept of *feeling*. Even those who have not read the concept in psychological terms, supposing it to refer merely to a

---

[15] *Ibid.*
[16] *Ibid.*, p. 22 (§5.3).
[17] It is interesting to find that Richard B. Brandt concludes, from an analysis of Schleiermacher's *Dialectic*, that, in this work at least, God appears as the genus which is the ground of all the species (*The Philosophy of Schleiermacher; the Development of His Theory of Scientific and Religious Knowledge*, New York: Harper & Bros., 1941, p. 238). But, while Schleiermacher did not always define God thus, he was consistent in his refusal to recognize the individual as a metaphysical unit. Brandt comments: "The reason why personal existence occurs at all is its revelation of the universe" (*ibid.*, p. 40).
[18] *The Christian Faith*, p. 26 (§6.1).

subjective emotion, have found it quite distressingly vague.[19] And vague it undoubtedly is. It may owe a good deal to Romanticism. (Rousseau's Vicar of Savoy, teaching that the promptings of the heart bring us into harmony with the will of God, affirmed, "*Nous sentons avant de connaître.*") A precise explanation will be sought in vain. We are told only that it is *conscious* feeling, and that psychology judges it to be an abiding-in-self (while *knowing* and *doing* involve passing-beyond-self). It is something of a paradox that Schleiermacher refrained from defining *feeling*, and yet increased its importance in his system by dropping the term *intuition*, which at first had been given an equal rank as a constituent of religion. This paradox is partly resolved, nevertheless, if we judge the concept against the background of Greek theology, and most especially in connection with the Greek *theoria*. Barth has pointed out how Schleiermacher believed that piety could never be correctly represented in words, so that its truth was best conveyed through poetry — or, beyond that, through wordless music — because the divine was ineffable.[20] Just so, the Greek view was that the highest truths could not be argued. Here *logos* (reasoning or rational discourse) was inappropriate and contemplation alone sufficed, in which the temporal gave way to the eternal, the human to the divine. What Schleiermacher called *piety* is, indeed, very close to Plato's understanding of philosophy (as he, a close student and translator of Plato, must have well realized); in each case, truth of a divine order is apprehended in a flight from the sensible world which liberates the divine in man. Only Schleiermacher could not make use of the Greek concept of *reason*, since the word had

[19] Brandt suggests that, just because Schleiermacher expressed himself without precision here, his views were the more influential (*The Philosophy of Schleiermacher*, p. 313). He himself says that it is reasonable to believe that the definition of religion as a feeling of dependence rests "upon the basis of his metaphysics, according to which God is the 'source' of all finite being" (*ibid.*, p. 252).

[20] *Protestant Thought from Rousseau to Ritschl*, pp. 335-36. The same theme is considered by Barth more fully in his essay, "Schleiermacher's 'Celebration of Christmas'" (Eng. trans. in *Theology and Church; Shorter Writings 1920-1928*, New York: Harper & Row, 1962, pp. 136-58).

been captured by the rationalists. The word *feeling*, on the other hand, conveyed the mystery of the depths (or heights) of spiritual awareness. So his concept of feeling combines the metaphysical and the mystical. It points to essential human nature, prior to the division of man into separate individuals possessing faculties adapted to the requirements of the sensible world. It declares man's essential unity with God, a unity which earthly existence may disrupt but cannot destroy. And it holds out the promise of an overcoming of disunity through a retreat from the merely sensual (and the merely rational, which serves the senses) to piety, feeling, awareness of our divinely grounded humanity — in short, to the mystery of Being.

For all his concern with philosophy, Schleiermacher remained preëminently a preacher and a theologian. But, having found revelation to be identical with God-consciousness, he was compelled to restate all theological propositions which had been formulated on the assumption that revelation was the divine Word received by faith. That meant adapting without exception the confessional statements of Protestantism. The record of the process of adaptation is contained in the great work of his maturity, *The Christian Faith*.

What is often overlooked is the quality of the doctrinal restatement Schleiermacher made, and so the implications of the changes he introduced are not adequately explored. We have to do with a radical transposition of the entire body of Christian doctrine into the world-view of immanence. Stated in post-Scholastic language, this means that the supernatural is absorbed into the natural; though *the natural* here is not naturalistically or empirically conceived but given a Romantic-mystical significance.[21] And the consequence of this disappearance of the

21 Schleiermacher speaks of *mysticism* in connection with his own outlook, using the word very broadly. Brandt suggests that he means by it "the view that only the whole is ultimately real," or "being lost in ecstatic rapture from insight into the world order," (*The Philosophy of Schleiermacher*, p. 102). The Romantic interpretation of *nature* normally assumed it to be a world order creating in man this kind of ecstatic re-

supernatural is that individual doctrines are no longer expositions of specific articles of belief but are turned into explanations
of how human nature is constituted and how it manifests its
divine ground. It is not the reception of the Gospel that is
discussed either, for the discussion turns on human consciousness considered as a Gospel in itself. Doctrinal restatement
shows (so the argument implicitly asserts) that Christianity is
an instrumental means to uncover the eternal truths about the
position of man in the universe.

As actually developed, Schleiermacher's account of why the
supernatural must be rejected is most informative and leads us
to the heart of his theological interpretation of Christianity. He
divided the question into two parts: the supernatural and the
supra-rational. And he connected it with "the appearance of
the Redeemer in history." This appearance, he argued, even
when regarded as the incarnation of the Son of God, was a
natural fact.

> For in the first place: as certainly as Christ was a man,
> there must reside in human nature the possibility of taking
> up the divine into itself, just as did happen in Christ. So that
> the idea that the divine revelation in Christ must in this
> respect be something absolutely supernatural will simply
> not stand the test.[22]

From the supernatural he turned to the supra-rational, saying
that "the supra-rational certainly has a place in the Redeemer
and the redeemed, and consequently in the whole compass of
Christianity."[23] The necessity for believing this came from the
fact that the redeemed possessed the indwelling of the divine,
and not all men were redeemed.

> But however great a difference we make between this supra-
> rational and the common human reason, it can never, with-

---

sponse. For a modern analysis of this side of Romanticism see *Romanticism Reconsidered*, ed. Northrop Frye (New York: Columbia Univ. Press,
1963).

[22] *The Christian Faith*, p. 64 (§13.1).
[23] *Ibid.*, p. 65 (§13.2).

out falling into self-contradiction, be set up as an *absolutely* supra-rational element. . . . Inasmuch . . . as the reason is completely one with the divine Spirit, the divine Spirit can itself be conceived as the highest enhancement of the human reason, so that the difference between the two is made to disappear.[24]

It is interesting to note that at this point Schleiermacher explicitly reproduced the Greek understanding of the full continuity existing between human reason and divine Spirit. But what is probably most illuminating is his emphasis upon the impossibility of anything *absolutely* supernatural or supra-rational. He was concerned to ban the supernatural and at the same time to gain recognition for a transcendental dimension of the natural — in other words, to establish the immanence of the divine. Consistently with this policy, therefore, he taught that even Christian piety, though partly supra-rational, was not unique in the universe. "For in the same sense in which the Christian self-consciousness is supra-rational," he wrote, "the whole of Nature is supra-rational too," — yet we called the processes of Nature purely rational.[25] And he summed up the matter thus.

> In one respect all Christian dogmas are supra-rational, in another they are all rational. They are supra-rational in the respect in which everything experiential is supra-rational. For there is an inner experience to which they may all be traced: they rest upon a *given;* and apart from this they could not have arisen, by deduction or synthesis, from universally recognized and communicable propositions.[26]

I have quoted Schleiermacher's own words fairly fully on this question, because his conclusions were not only crucial for setting the orientation of his own restatement of Christian doctrines but also had an extraordinarily wide influence on the subsequent history of Protestant theology. From his belief that the inner

24 *Ibid.*
25 *Ibid.*, p. 66 (§13. *Postscript*).
26 *Ibid.*, p. 67 (§13. *Postscript*).

experience of Christian believers is supra-rational and yet given, for instance, there followed a long series of apologetic theologies reared on the supposition that Christianity could be proven true because it had an unassailable "empirical" foundation in the believer's experience.[27] Yet there can be no doubt that the pivotal point of his interpretation of Christianity is easy to recognize, if we are on the alert for it. And it can be seen in the terms in which the absolutely supernatural is dismissed.

Because Christ was a man, "there must reside in human nature the possibility of taking up the divine into itself, just as did happen in Christ," Schleiermacher argues. The argument is a kind of Chinese nest-of-boxes of assumptions. First, Schleiermacher assumes that Christ took up the divine into his human nature. Next, he assumes that Christ had one "nature" and that nature was a human one. Finally, he assumes that human nature is a constant, so that we can generalize from one instance to all, from Christ to humanity. The Christological assumptions here obviously run counter to Chalcedonian Christology, which formed the background to the Protestant confessional formulae which *The Christian Faith* purported to interpret. And, just as obviously, Schleiermacher's Christology is fitted into his metaphysical theory that the divine is the ground of all finite being, but comes to self-consciousness in human nature.

The metaphysical frame of Schleiermacher's whole approach is even indicated in his phrase "the appearance of the Redeemer in history." History might be thought to be the realm of the sensible, from which a metaphysician would turn away in order to immerse himself in the real. But history could also be viewed as the place where the ground of the Whole revealed itself, because through the individual events of the historical scene a pattern could be discerned which indicated the nature of the Whole. This latter vision of history was being glimpsed, before the end of the eighteenth century, by such thinkers as Herder and Friedrich Schlegel, and Schleiermacher developed the vision

[27] See below, Part Three.

and passed it on.[28] It brought with it novel themes — development, evolutionary progress, and dynamic process — quite different from the static categories of Greek thought; but the new and the old were fused together in Schleiermacher's thought. He was able to keep his basic belief in the eternal, infinite Being, the changeless ground of the finite, and yet account for the appearance of the unprecedented: for example, Christianity. Revelation was always itself (the coming into consciousness of the dependence of the finite on the infinite). Nevertheless, Christianity meant the disclosure of a fresh starting-point for revelation. It meant looking to one man, with whom the revelation decisively began, and speaking of *the appearance of the Redeemer in history*. Such was the background against which Schleiermacher introduced his doctrinal restatements, and, in particular, his Christological restatements. When we look for the meaning he gave to his verbal creations, we can see that he has caught them all like flies in the web of his metaphysic. Thus "an appearance in history" is not for him merely the arrival of something new in the sensible world but also a clue to the divinity which is the source of all.

It will be necessary to look a little further into Schleiermacher's interpretation of the historical, since Christianity is so closely bound up with historical events.

Schleiermacher loses no time in explaining that the entry of the Founder of Christianity onto the historical scene points to a completely general lesson about man in the universe.

> . . . the appearing of such a life is the result of the power of development which resides in our human nature — a power which expresses itself in particular men at particular points according to laws which, if hidden from us, are nevertheless of divine arrangement, in order through these men to help the others forward. And indeed, apart from

[28] Brandt refers to Theodor Haering's opinion that Schleiermacher's idea of the process of history being a revelation of the universe may have influenced Hegel (*The Philosophy of Schleiermacher*, p. 141).

such a supposition, any progress of the human race as a whole or any part of it would be inconceivable.[29]

Thus it seems that no supernatural act of God was involved when God sent his Son into the world. Natural laws (but divine too, as everything in Nature is natural-divine) account completely for the Incarnation. Incarnation must be reckoned an innate possibility in human nature. Incarnation also, while marking a decisive stage in world-development, is seen to happen in order to advance an evolutionary pattern: "He alone is destined gradually to quicken the whole human race into higher life."[30] In the series of events recounted by scripture and recalled in the creeds — Christ's birth, crucifixion, resurrection, and ascension — Schleiermacher takes no serious interest. For him Christian faith is not related to a historical life (Jesus of Nazareth) except as that life is taken to mark the "appearance" in the temporal of an eternal truth about human nature. On that account, he defines faith in Christ as "the certainty that the influence of Christ puts an end to the state of being in need of redemption, and produces that other state [of the higher self-consciousness]."[31] He adds that this faith "is a purely factual certainty, but a certainty of a fact which is entirely inward."[32] In other words, we turn to history in order to be able to turn away from history, looking at the outward simply to penetrate to the inward. Or history is a screen upon which the features of the immanent God are projected; and we need the screen to carry the image. The historical life of the Redeemer is the occasion for launching the influence of his appearance as Redeemer (or Quickener of the higher self-consciousness), which thereafter remains as a permanent feature of the universe.

The function of history, in such a view, seems to be to act as a medium by means of which the infinite reveals itself in the infinite and the temporal manifests the eternal. It is not a

[29] *Ibid.*, p. 63 (§13.1).
[30] *Ibid.*
[31] *Ibid.*, p. 68 (§14.1).
[32] *Ibid.*

matter of the infinite coming into the finite — for it is there already, as the source and ground of all finite being — but of its progressive self-disclosure there. My metaphor of the screen might be extended, therefore, by imagining that the features of the immanent God become continually clearer as they are brought into focus. We have only to imagine that this is achieved by an adjustment of the screen, which moves so as to bring about the sharpening of the image by stages. The way in which history provides the necessary medium for the infinite to disclose itself is exemplified by Schleiermacher in his explanation of the meaning of the Church. His concept of a *Church*, like his concept of *revelation* and his concept of a *Redeemer*, is completely general in its basic reference. A Church is a

> . . . relatively closed religious communion, which forms an ever self-renewing circulation of the religious self-consciousness within certain definite limits, and a propagation of the religious emotions arranged and organized within the same limits, so that there can be some kind of definite understanding as to which individuals belong to it and which do not. . . .[33]

Why is a Church necessary? Because, says Schleiermacher, there is no such thing as *religion in general*, except as a general tendency in the human soul. Religion manifests itself in the world by individuals' joining together in fellowships. What we always find in the world are Churches, embodying different levels or stages of religious self-consciousness, and creating the various religions of mankind.

Once again, we find in Schleiermacher's teaching his belief that the reality of the individual is his participation in a species, his being united to a whole. So the various religions at any one level are actually compared to species within a genus. At the apex of all religions stands Christianity, born of the Church (i.e. the corporate Christian consciousness). It represents the

[33] *Ibid.*, p. 29 (§6.2).

gradual emergence of truth out of truth-mixed-with-error, being the final stage in the realization of the innate tendency of human nature. Just so, in the realm of Nature, we recognize perfect and imperfect animals as different stages of the development of animal life.[34]

The Church which gives birth to the Christian religion is thus itself the product of a universe which develops in accordance with the "movements of the divine Spirit" immanent within it. If that Spirit dwells in the Church preserving there the continuous influence of Christ, this is only because "the human reason in a sense contains that which is produced by the divine Spirit," — as is proved by man's consciousness of his need of redemption outside Christianity as well as inside it.[35] The Church is the historical consequence of the "temporal appearance" of the Redeemer. But the Redeemer's appearance is simply a moment in the "universal spiritual life." The act of taking up the divine into the human accomplished in his person is to be understood as "an action of human nature, grounded in its original constitution and prepared for by all its past history, and accordingly as the highest development of its spiritual power."[36] It follows that the moment of highest development is significant only in the context of the universal spiritual life. Schleiermacher may insist upon the unique role played by the Redeemer, claiming that, "in comparison with Him, everything which could otherwise be regarded as revelation again loses this character."[37] Yet the fact remains that he has made the original constitution of human nature all-important, so that the Redeemer can do no more than manifest in time an eternal reality. Historically regarded, Christians owe their faith to Christ's influence perpetuated in the Church. But the truth of the situation is that, over and beyond history, hu-

---

[34] *Ibid.*, p. 33 (§7.3).
[35] *Ibid.*, p. 65(§13.2).
[36] *Ibid.*, p. 64 (§13.1).
[37] *Ibid.*, p. 63 (§13.1).

man nature obeys the laws of its own constitution, since anything else would be unthinkable. History is nothing but a moment-by-moment revelation of the structure of the universe, faith is properly an internal certainty and a necessity of human nature, and Christ is individuality deriving from pure general human nature uncontaminated by the sensuous.

The world-view outlined in the Introduction to *The Chrisian Faith* set the pattern for the detailed restatements of Protestant doctrines given through the rest of the work. Schleiermacher was a consistent expositor. Although I take up a few of his characteristic conclusions in the next chapter of the present enquiry, there is no need to spell these out in detail. Once the metaphysical inspiration which unites them all within a common frame is recognized, they occasion very little perplexity. What the reader of *The Christian Faith* is likely to note in addition to its internal consistency, however, is the sense of assured and easy control of its material which it conveys. And that virtue — still evident to us today — made it so extraordinarily influential in its own century. The Jericho walls of traditional theological language had been demolished; and Christian doctrine, freed from the jargon of the schools, seemed ready now to occupy the whole Promised Land of contemporary culture.

No little part of his success followed from the lack of formal precision in his definitions and, especially, from the ambiguity of his central concept of feeling. It is true that the propositions contained in the opening chapter of *The Christian Faith* had been labelled "Propositions borrowed from Ethics," "Propositions borrowed from the Philosophy of Religion," "Propositions borrowed from Apologetics." But there had been no systematic setting out of philosophical presuppositions and no detailed metaphysical argument. His world-view was close enough to others formulated around that time to permit an assimilation of his teaching to the teachings of other philosophers and philosophical theologians: for example, Hegel.[38] On that account, many acknowledged themselves to be convinced by his general approach to religion, praised his "insights," adopted the majority of his doctrinal formulae, and yet went on to explain that he had not really achieved a solid foundation upon which to establish the truth of Christianity.

It was out of the "Yes, but . . ." reaction to Schleiermacher that there developed the theological outlook which we have come to call *liberalism*. Although this name was at first attached to German theologians who thought of themselves as Schleiermacher's Left, in our own century it became an inclusive label distinguishing "progressive" religious thinking from "reactionary." The practical touchstone for finding out where theological liberalism divided from theological conservatism was the critical interpretation of the Bible. By denying the distinction between the natural and the supernatural, Schleiermacher had bypassed the position held by the orthodox of his day, assuming that Scripture, having supernatural authority, must be inerrant and not subject to human canons of criticism. In this, as in other matters relating to "modern thought," where the influence of the theology of feeling was extended, there the friction between religion and secular culture was reduced or entirely abolished. Consequently, conservative religious opinion complained about the way in which *modernism* was eroding the fundamentals of the faith. The large element of truth in the conservative complaint did not strike home to the liberal camp for a long time. There were two reasons for this. First, the freedom which theology had gained by breaking with eighteenth-century orthodoxy and making use of the resources of

[38] In an Appendix entitled "Schleiermacher and Hegel," Brandt discusses the personal antagonism which divided these two thinkers and also led Hegel to criticize the theology of feeling so strongly. However, after contrasting their views of religion and philosophy, feeling and reason, Brandt concludes: "The differences between them here were not clear-cut logical disagreements but more matters of temperament and emphasis — differences which however have been historically decisive, as is clear from the development of German thought after their time" (*The Philosophy of Schleiermacher*, p. 326).

nineteenth-century culture (especially of the growing understanding of historical method) was a solid achievement and an
exhilarating one. Second, while the liberals were largely blind
to the incompatibility of their (often unconscious) metaphysical
presuppositions and biblical basis of the Gospel, they were
realistic in their perception that the conservatives had a false
notion of the cause they championed. For the latter, claiming
to defend the Bible from its enemies, in fact were defending
a rationalistic theological approach derived from Protestant
scholasticism, in the categories of which they interpreted both
the authority and the contents of scripture. Thus the liberals
were able to reply, with some justification, that they stood for
the life-bringing spirit and not the dead letter.

Liberalism stood for more, however, than freedom from the
theological limitations of reactionary orthodoxy. The theologians
of Schleiermacher's Left had contrasted the Christ of history
with the Christ of faith. That this focus of interest became
more intense through the first decades of the twentieth century
was no doubt the result of a growing tendency to move from
transcendentalism to empiricism (and from "universal history"
to concrete historical studies). This shift of interest eventually
led to the dethronement of Hegel in philosophy. But the theological influence here was, above all, that of Albrecht Ritschl.
Liberal Protestantism, most particularly in its Anglo-Saxon form,
stems from his influence.[39]

For "the Christ of faith" can be taken in two senses. It
can be taken to refer to the Christ of the historic creeds. Or
it can be taken to refer to (and, indeed, it was sometimes written thus) "the ideal Christ." In the second sense it applies to

---

[39] Barth, oddly, belittles Ritschl's influence, describing his teaching
merely as a reaction, a return to the Enlightenment (*Protestant Thought
from Rousseau to Ritschl*, pp. 390-97). Brunner describes him as "the
second milestone" in nineteenth-century theology (Eng. trans., *The
Mediator*, London: Lutterworth Press, 1934, p. 56). Kenneth Cauthen in
The Impact of American Religious Liberalism (New York: Harper & Row,
1962) mentions Schleiermacher and Ritschl together as "tremendously influential" (p. 19).

Schleiermacher's description of the Redeemer. Now, Ritschl was opposed to Schleiermacher's "mysticism." He followed him in believing that doctrines could do no more than indicate what was contained in man's religious experience. Yet he held that the response to the revelation of God in Christ had as its result not simply a change in man's internal consciousness but specifically an ethical advance in history. "The Christ of history," then, was a concept supporting Ritschlian practicality; while, by comparison, the Redeemer-Christ of Schleiermacher seemed a theoretical construct. The trans-natural had begun to look as outmoded as the supernatural. Actually, Ritschl's vision of Christ as the bearer of God's moral lordship over men and as the founder of the Kingdom of God was equally theoretical. His famous "value-judgments" were only "the higher self-consciousness" lifted into the moral sphere. But this vision, because it related faith to the external world of human activity instead of to the nonsensible world of the universal spiritual life, appealed to a generation which was moving away from idealism in the direction of realism. Schleiermacher had insisted that, although Christianity begannhistorically with Jesus of Nazareth, yet it was founded on the experienced reality of Jesus as the Christ representing general human nature. Ritschl opened the way for liberalism to concentrate upon Jesus as an ethical personality who showed us how to live in loving trust in a God who willed for us only good. A rash of "lives" of Jesus, leaning heavily on the synoptic Gospels and ignoring the "speculative" passages in the New Testament, showed that his lesson had been well learned.[40]

Schleiermacher remarked that an emphasis upon the redeeming work of Christ accompanied belief in the distinctive nature

[40] T. R. Glover's *The Jesus History* (London: S.C.M., 1917), which in many ways typifies the religious interests of its era, is actually quite "right wing" in its doctrinal standpoint. It attempts to present a fully human Jesus, who, nevertheless, can be discovered to be the Christ of faith. Glover minimizes the supernatural in connection with the ministry of Jesus, but he does not exclude it entirely. He insists, for instance, that this ministry cannot be understood apart from the resurrection.

of Christian piety, whereas the emphasis upon Christ as primarily a teacher and organizer of a communion went with the view of Christianity as primarily one form of religion in general.[41] He himself adopted the first pair of related teachings; and Ritschl, by adopting the second, showed that he had strayed — by Schleiermacher's standards — into heresy. Ritschl's theology revolved around Christ's preaching of the Kingdom of God, and, by its denigration of *the mystical* and its exaltation of *the practical,* shifted the center of concern from redemption to "establishing the Kingdom." As one of the early interpreters of Ritschlianism to the English-speaking world commented:

> While the Kingdom of God is conceived by Ritschl as not only a moral ideal, a social organization of mankind from the motive of love, but as also a religious good, an individual possession assured to faith; yet the immanent logic of the term is stronger than its formal definition, and what we practically find is that the moral duty pushes itself to the front, and the religious good falls into the background.[42]

In liberalism this logic was taken to its limit in the Social Gospel.[43] The result was an immeasurable advance in ethical understanding within the Church beyond the individualistic other-worldliness which had become the cultural pattern of Protestant conservatism. There was a rediscovery of the realism of the Bible in its emphasis upon social righteousness. At the

[41] *The Christian Faith,* p. 57 (§11.4). See also his defense of the *mystical* view of redemption as over against the *empirical* view (*ibid.*, pp. 428-31, §100.3).

[42] Alfred E. Garvie, *The Ritschlian Theology, Critical and Constructive* (Edinburgh: T. & T. Clark, 1899), p. 251. Garvie had been discussing Ritschl's definition of Christianity as "an ellipse, ruled by two foci" — redemption and the moral organization of humanity by love.

[43] Cauthen says that Walter Rauschenbusch "had both the mystical tendencies of Schleiermacher and the ethical tendencies of Ritschl," (*The Impact of American Religious Liberalism,* p. 88). But the core of Rauschenbusch's theology was unquestionably the Kingdom of God read in Ritschlian terms.

same time, everything was seen from the perspective of immanence; and so Christianity was turned into a message of social idealism, with Christ as the perfect social legislator. At bottom, this was no more than a variant of Ritschl's transposition of Schleiermacher's theology from the realm of Being into the realm of action. Instead of being pure general human nature, Jesus was the inspiration of "a divine social order established on earth."[44] If the latter assertion is pressed (as post-Ritschlians, because of their "practical" outlook, neglected to press their statements) it appears that Jesus was the first manifestation of a pure general social will immanent in human history.[45]

The old natural theology had been the result of faith in the universality and permanence of reason. Reason, speaking through the metaphysician, conveyed objective truth about the source and ground of all things. So natural theology was a theology of genuine intelligibility. When Schleiermacher shifted the locus of theological certainty from reason to feeling (i.e. self-consciousness), he effected the transition to a Theology of Meaningfulness. What was now of first importance was not that we understood conceptually but that we felt satisfied, fulfilled, and at one with the ground of our being and meaning. Ritschl preferred value-judgments to "mystical" consciousness of self-within-the-whole, and put relevance ahead even of meaning. He found support in an age that was confident that it knew what it wanted and took for granted the soundness of its judgments.

> The conviction is growing and spreading that religion is worth saving and keeping, if not for its own sake, yet at least on account of the services it has rendered, and may yet be expected to render, to mankind in its moral and social progress. . . . A new demand is thus made upon religion. Can it not only assure man of his individual

[44] The phrase is Rauschenbusch's, quoted by Cauthen (*ibid.*, p. 89).
[45] Cauthen also quotes Rauschenbusch's dictum that Jesus is "the type of Man as he is to be," (*ibid.*, p. 105).

salvation, but also secure for mankind its social regeneration?[46]

New questions were being asked, but they were being asked before the same shrine. An indubitable answer was still expected from religion as found immanent in the human spirit. And the earthbound God was believed to be about to confirm his answer in the final development of the historical progress. Ritschl's "heretical" or "deviationist" theology was firmly rooted within the immanentist "orthodoxy" of Schleiermacher.

[46] Garvie, *The Ritschlian Theology*, pp. 4, 17. Garvie, incidentally, was a "right wing" Ritschlian. He did not believe that relevance was the sole criterion of a Christian theology.

6

Schleiermacher's Modern Sons

THE DISADVANTAGE OF FOUNDING A THEOLOGY UP-
on relevance is that it may suddenly become irrelevant and
die. This is what happened to post-Ritschlian liberal theology
after the First World War; although it did not happen over-
night, and death was less the result of a lethal blow than of prolonged exposure to an unfriendly environment. Here and there
are to be found those who argue that the exposure has not
proved fatal and that liberalism is strong and will be stronger.
Yet the truth of the matter would seem to be that the brand of
liberalism which arose out of the practical and social emphasis
of Ritschl's teaching and which was challenged, first by Barth
and a little later by Reinhold Niebuhr, did not survive the
Second World War. Ritschlian liberalism lived out of a conviction that it had discovered the only possible Christian gospel for the enlightened contemporary conscience; and, once its
self-confidence had been shaken, it ceased to be a creative force
maintaining its own life. Hencefore it could survive simply
in the lives of those who had known it while it was still a vital,
missionary cause; or else it must be re-born — as *neo*-liberalism.

The latter course was always open, naturally. And it was to be expected especially if, as I have argued, post-Ritschlian liberalism was no more than a "heresy" within a wider "orthodoxy," a variation of a larger theological movement.

Such an explanation seems to be borne out by a recent defense of liberalism by a distinguished supporter of that outlook who has never wavered in his allegiance: Henry P. van Dusen.[1] The defense is one which undoubtedly does *not* present some neo-liberalism but takes its stand upon authentic liberalism of early twentieth-century vintage. So much can be seen in Van Dusen's explanation that the evangelical liberalism he supports is the declaration of a conviction, "at once credible to the Mind of Today and yet in unmistakable and unchallengeable continuity with *true* Christian Faith, i.e. the faith of Jesus of Nazareth."[2] Yet where today would he find support for his contention that the Synoptic Gospels give us glimpses of "the *true* Jesus," while Acts and Paul's letters reflect the badly distorted ideas about him prevailing in the primitive Church?[3] The point here is not, as Van Dusen apparently takes it to be, that liberalism stands confirmed if only certain skeptical trends in modern New Testament scholarship concerning the portrait of Jesus of Nazareth in the Gospels are overcome. The point is that — granted the substantial accuracy of the Synoptic portrait — the liberal attempt to extract the *true* Jesus as a human being of surpassing worth hidden behind an artificially contrived God-man now seems to be an expenditure of energy in the service of a lost cause.

[1] *The Vindication of Liberal Theology, a Tract for the Times* (New York: Scribner's Sons, 1963).

[2] *Ibid.*, p. 24.

[3] *Ibid.*, pp. 118-22. In genuinely Ritschlian style, Van Dusen argues that the Synoptics give us the real Jesus because they alone stress the Kingdom of God (*ibid.*, p. 122). Earlier he had quoted with approval from C. H. Dodd's *The Apostolic Preaching and its Development,* concluding that "the first Christians had a single message for the world; it was a message of Jesus Christ," (*ibid.*, p. 94). But it turns out that their message cannot be trusted, for we have to disentangle the *true* message from the distorted record left by the Church.

For the fact of the matter is that Van Dusen argues from Ritschlian value-judgments which are no longer convincing or relevant to contemporary problems. For example, he ends his vindication of liberalism by telling us what the content of Christian doctrine should be.[4] The doctrine of man (so he argues) should be based on the "largely unuttered" assumptions of the outlook of Jesus, and will probably find no place for original sin. The doctrine of God needs no other category than "Father." Christology "need not go beyond Jesus' own declarations of his nature and his vocation; more or other than these forever threaten distortion of his true Reality." Finally, the norm of doctrine is not to be found in our own theories of reality but in "the only concept which commanded Jesus' absolute loyalty — the *Kingdom of God*." "Here, it will be agreed," says Van Dusen, "is a searching, purging, asceptic test."

Here, on the contrary, are all Ritschl's well-worn themes: the exclusion of metaphysics, denial of original sin, a merely fatherly God, Christ known through his vocation, the Kingdom of God as God's supreme purpose and Christ's personal purpose. Here also, therefore, is the confusion at the heart of Ritschl's "practical" outlook. If theories of reality are outlawed, it is odd that we should meet at every turn statements about reality together with exhortations to separate what is true from what is distorted interpretation.

Of course, Van Dusen believes that the foundation of the liberal value-judgment is firm. It is the norm of liberal theology. "Liberal theology locates the decisive norm at one place: the mind and especially the faith of Jesus."[5] But how, we may then ask, do we *know* the mind and the faith of Jesus? How do we look into the New Testament and discern there in the record about Jesus what Van Dusen calls "his true Reality" from distortions of it? It is at this point that Ritschlianism shows itself to be dependent, for all its differences, upon Schleiermacher's metaphysical views. The value-judgment about Jesus

[4] *Ibid.*, pp. 147f.
[5] *Ibid.*, p. 93.

is rooted in a theology of immanence, and denial of the supernatural, or in "the principle of continuity."[6] So Van Dusen
tells us that a general interpretation of reality will admit neither
unqualified continuity nor total discontinuity, i.e. "continuity
with real differences."[7] But continuity is "total" between the
human Jesus and the divine Christ.[8] In other words, it is
necessary, after all, to hold a particular theory of reality.
(Van Dusen, in fact, believes in the Universe as an evolving
process leading to *spirit*, basing his belief on the teachings of
"the most competent scientists, philosophers and theologians
of the last generation,"[9] — he does not mention either Schleiermacher or Hegel.) On the basis of this theory we can go
on to decide what we shall choose as the marks of the *true*
Christian faith setting forth the *true* Jesus. We can know the
mind and faith of Jesus because it is essentially our own mind
and faith. We can build on the impression we have of the
self-consciousness of Jesus because it is an impression of a
self-consciousness continuous with ours, and because we find
our highest aspirations fulfilled in him.

Barth's revolt against liberalism was so decisive chiefly because it struck right at the heart of its adversary. Barth did
not stop with the externals of liberalism which were the legacy
of Ritschl — its this-worldliness, its moral and social emphasis,
or its claim to have discovered the Christ of history. Instead,
he moved in to attack its theory of reality. Since the Christian
Gospel is a message about the acts of a transcendent God, this
message could not be proclaimed within a framework of im-
manency. Thus Barth moved to reverse the whole movement of
nineteenth-century Protestant theology. As he said later, looking back to the days of the revolt: "The ship was threatening to
run aground; the moment was at hand to turn the rudder an

[6] *Ibid.*, pp. 83f. Van Dusen finds this latter term used by John C.
Bennett and by Kenneth Cauthen.
[7] *Ibid.*, pp. 88f.
[8] *Ibid.*, p. 89.
[9] *Ibid*, pp. 83f.

angle of exactly 180 degrees. . . . There never could be a question of denying or reversing that change."[10] So he was not content simply to oppose current teaching (for instance, that of his old teacher, Adolf Harnack). He went straight to the fountainhead of doctrine, to the source of the liberal tradition, to Schleiermacher's identification of Christ with general human nature. Over against the faith in immanence he set the declaration that God was the Wholly Other and the insistence that salvation came down from heaven in a (supernatural) vertical line meeting the horizontal line of the life of humanity (the "down here"). It was a specific denial of the earthbound God.

Barth's singling out of Schleiermacher as *the* theologian who had set the course for the ship of theology over more than a century was linked with his very great admiration for that theologian, his insights and his creative power. When the impact of Barth's revolt began to be felt, however, what was felt most keenly was less his theological analysis than his repudiation of current liberal values. "Neo-orthodoxy" seemed to be a movement dedicated to turning men away from the humanism and this-worldliness of liberalism and from a preoccupation with the Christ of history. So such thinkers as Reinhold Niebuhr and Paul Tillich, who criticized modern Protestantism for reflecting uncritically a shallow secular culture and who suggested that classic Christian dogma was more than a distortion of the simple teachings of Jesus, were at first considered by American liberals to be Barthians. It took some time for people to grasp that to wish to alter the course of the ship of theology was not necessarily to intend to have it sail in the opposite direction.

Meanwhile, Barth's uncompromising teachings grew in influence. Emil Brunner helped to introduce the "theology of Crisis" to the Anglo-Saxon world, and Reinhold Niebuhr crusaded against liberal illusions over man's perfectibility. Under the impact, especially, of Niebuhr's attacks upon moralistic Christianity and utopian perfectionism, liberalism soon became

[10] "*Die Menschlichkeit Gottes*," Eng. trans. in *The Humanity of God* (Richmond, Virginia: John Knox Press, 1960), p. 41.

"chastened" (to use Walter Marshall Horton's expressive term),
acknowledging that it had been too optimistic, too culture-con-
scious, and too little mindful of traditional Christian doctrine, in
its views of man. But it by no means became converted to
Barthianism. So chastened liberals, being ready for a change,
though not for a full-scale revolution, settled for what was essentially a palace revolution. In effect, they repudiated Ritschlian heresy and fell back upon the orthodoxy out of which it
had originally arisen; and "neo-liberalism" was born.

To speak of "neo-liberalism" is to use a very general term,
of course. Yet it is a useful way of describing a theologian such
as Niebuhr who, after half a life-time of attacking liberalism,
confesses to being "a liberal at heart."[11] A conspicuous mark
of neo-liberalism is the use of the argument that the way through
for theology today is one avoiding the extremes of both liberalism and orthodoxy. The wish to steer a middle course turns out
to be the determination to cling to a theology of immanence,
coupled with a retreat from the anti-metaphysical pretensions
of the Christ-of-history-and-the-Gospels school. Consciously or
unconsciously, neo-liberals rally under the banner of Schleiermacher.

There is a near identity apparent in many present-day theologies which are superficially quite unlike, a basic similarity
issuing from the fact that their creators are building upon the
foundations laid by Schleiermacher and re-using materials he
gathered. The evidence here is both abundant and striking. I
will limit myself in this chapter to looking at three major assumptions which neo-liberals share with Schleiermacher and
which show their theologies to be largely republications of his.
These assumptions arise in connection with (1) the starting-
point of theology in human self-consciousness, (2) the basis of
Christology in human nature, and (3) the understanding of

---

[11] Quoting Niebuhr here, Van Dusen finds his "recantation" an "ideal
stance" from which to reassess liberalism's "validity and importance for
tomorrow." (*The Vindication of Liberal Theology*, pp. 54f.). Surely
recantation is much too strong a word for Niebuhr's confession.

history as a progressive revelation of the structure of the universe.

Strangely enough, few of Schleiermacher's modern sons are ready to acknowledge him as their spiritual father.

(1)

Daniel Day William's *God's Grace and Man's Hope*[12] illustrates very well the foundation of neo-liberalism in the theology of feeling. Williams declares his purpose in writing to be to establish a "structurally sound theology," neither neo-orthodox nor liberal.[13] And he proceeds to give us his doctrinal approach to the knowledge of God: "The God who is present to us can be known through our direct experience of Him. This is a radical assertion. It establishes the resemblance of our standpoint to some types of Christian thought, and cuts us off sharply from others."[14] He does not specify the conflicting types of Christian thought he has in mind, and Schleiermacher's name is not once mentioned in the whole book. Yet his concentration upon experience as the source of all religious reality is a silent witness to his indebtedness to the theology of feeling, while other supporting elements of his thought point the same way. Like Schleiermacher, he thinks of godlessness as God-forgetfulness, putting forward the prime condition of recognizing the presence of God as being a state of "sensitive discrimination and responsiveness" (called by Schleiermacher "the vitality of the higher self-consciousness"). Like Schleiermacher, too, he finds his final authority for Christian doctrine in the experience of the Christian community regarded as a channel of human consciousness.

Williams argues that our experience of God's presence is not our own doing, since it is the activity of God in us. "All knowledge of God that is recognition — and not merely

[12] New York: Harper Bros., 1949.
[13] *Ibid.*, p. 11. He puts Niebuhr together with the neo-orthodox theologians.
[14] *Ibid.*, p. 45.

cognition — of His reality, is a gift which is given by the working of God himself in our life."[15] This may seem to be an admission of the otherness of God; but actually it is an expression, in time-honored terms, of the theology of immanence. It ties in with the belief that, God being the ground of our self-consciousness, we can never be more than partially forgetful of the divine; and so our knowledge of God — our original knowledge which is to be distinguished from our rational deductions from the given — is not a new discovery but a remembering. As Kierkegaard pointed out long ago, all theories of recollection (from Plato onward) assume that man himself is part of the divine consciousness, for otherwise God's working in man to stimulate knowledge of divinity cannot be identified with human experience.[16]

Kierkegaard was one of the first to notice the significance of the nineteenth-century revolt against supernaturalism and to trace it to its theological starting-point. He insisted that to argue from man's capacity for spirituality was to miss the point of Christianity. He distinguished between *Religiousness A* (the religion of immanence) and *Religiousness B* (Christianity), making the distinction in order to show that Christian faith could not be identified with the findings of our God-consciousness.[17] And he commented: "What Schleiermacher calls 'Religion' and the Hegelians 'Faith' is at bottom nothing but the first immediate condition for everything — the vital fluidum — the spiritual atmosphere we breathe in — and which cannot therefore with justice be designated by those words."[18] The relevance of Kierkegaard's distinction is made plain when we find Williams defining God as "that reality in and through all things which makes possible the response of life to the lure

15 *Ibid.*, p. 50.
16 *Philosophical Fragments* (Princeton: Princeton Univ. Press, 1962), pp. 10ff.
17 *Concluding Unscientific Postscript* (Princeton: Princeton Univ. Press, 1941), pp. 493ff.
18 *The Journals of Sören Kierkegaard*, edited by Alexander Dru (London: Oxford University Press, 1938), 78.

of fulfillment beyond the present."[19] To appeal to this God is, after all, to refer simply to a spiritual force immanent in the universe. If this earthbound God is to be identified with the God of Christian revelation, it must be by assuming that there can be no other God, since the earthbound God is metaphysically indubitable. *He* alone is God, and metaphysics has declared him.

Any theology starting from human experience or self-consciousness must rest, in fact, upon a metaphysical theory. Schleiermacher was able to contend that his theology was not speculative only because he separated feeling from reason. Yet he had first comprehended the two within one all-embracing whole. In his recent study of Schleiermacher, Richard R. Niebuhr explains the master's outlook thus: "Philosophy and religion are each entirely original manifestations of human nature, the one of reason seeking knowledge, the other of feeling disclosing man's dependence."[20] Niebuhr, however, does not stop to observe that such an outlook presupposes that we know indubitably what are original manifestations of human nature and that these manifestations are the necessary gateways to truth. Today, neo-liberalism branches out into different varieties of "philosophical theology" claiming to meet alike the requirements of philosophy and religion. Many definitions of God follow. Thus, H. Richard Niebuhr advocates a "radical monotheism" based on "reliance on the source of all being for the significance of the self and of all that exists" — a faith designed to satisfy the "believing self" and the "reasoning self."[21] Nels Ferré thinks that twentieth-century knowledge can give content to faith in God as "love, made known . . . in concerned, creative, and co-operative community."[22] Paul Tillich

[19] *Op. cit.*, p. 51.
[20] *Schleiermacher on Christ and Religion; A New Interpretation* (New York: Scribner's Sons, 1964), p. 171.
[21] *Radical Monotheism and Western Culture, with Supplementary Essays* (New York: Harper & Brothers, 1960), pp. 32f.
[22] *Searchlights on Contemporary Theology* (New York: Harper & Brothers, 1961), p. 183.

develops his "method of correlation" (intended to unite faith and knowledge) against the background of faith conceived as ultimate concern about our being and meaning.[23]

Among neo-liberals Tillich is the one who has most to say about his debt to Schleiermacher.[24] Nevertheless, it is apparent that modern philosophical theology generally is developed under the shadow of Schleiermacher, making God-consciousness its common starting-point. Everywhere within this perspective we discover that Kierkegaard's *Religiousness A* makes its appearance. The perspective is one of immanence, for, although the definitions of God advanced may contain the word *transcendent,* they actually refer to a deity immanent within experience and transcendent only as the ground of experience. So Williams finds God to be the source of the drive of all things toward their fulfillment; H. Richard Niebuhr finds him to be that from which all selves derive their significance; Ferré finds him to be the love-power proven in community; and Tillich finds him to be the ground and abyss of the Being which we are aware of in all that exists. For these thinkers the actual objects of faith are: the drive for self-fulfillment, the consciousness of human significance, the response-in-love to community, and Being-conveyed-through-awareness. When God is "discovered" in these things, he is needed simply in order to guarantee their abiding reality. In other words, philosophical theology extracts God from the place where he is immanently dwelling, explaining his nature by means of the place of his indwelling. Such a God is indubitable if the metaphysical arguments used to establish him are fully cogent. But, in that case, we are left with an earthbound God — a "that which" — who is certainly not the transcendent God who revealed himself to Israel and spoke finally in the person of his Incarnate Son. A theology

---

23 *Systematic Theology,* I, 8, 14.
24 Tillich admits that Schleiermacher's "feeling of absolute dependence" is similiar to his own "ultimate concern" (*ibid.,* p. 42). Nels Ferré (*Searchlights,* p. 90n.) reports that, in conversation, Tillich said that Schleiermacher was his "spiritual father."

which has God-consciousness for its starting-point cannot advance beyond self-certainty in order to speak of a God of revelation, a God who is more than an echo of humanity itself.

(2)

To ask whether or not a definition of God is compatible with Christian faith is necessarily to ask how it relates to the Lordship of Jesus Christ. Schleiermacher solved the problem of linking faith in experience (the experience of God-consciousness innate in general human nature) with Christian faith in Jesus Christ the Incarnate Son of God by presenting Jesus as the archetypal human being in whom our potential human experience was actually realized. Confessing that in Jesus we see God Incarnate seemed to Schleiermacher no difficult task, "for to ascribe to Christ an absolutely powerful God-consciousness, and to attribute to Him an existence of God in Him, are exactly the same thing."[25] This same solution is adopted by the neo-liberals, who find that Emmanuel was the clearest (and hence the decisive) embodiment of divinity accessible to humanity. He is "history's Most High" — to use a favorite expression of Ferré. In this view there are three prime assumptions.

The first assumption is that incarnation is no unique event, but a normal and constantly repeated pattern in the immanence of the divine within things terrestrial. An implication of this assumption is that there can be many "sons" of God found in the natural course of history.

In keeping with this usage, H. Richard Niebuhr writes: "We may use the theological word 'incarnation' in speaking of the coming of radically monotheistic faith into our history, meaning by it the concrete expression in a total life of radical trust in the One and of universal loyalty to the realm of being."[26] He goes on to describe the incarnation of radical faith in the people of Israel, concluding: "Jesus Christ represents the incarna-

---

[25] *The Christian Faith,* pp. 386-87 (§94.2).
[26] *Radical Monotheism,* p. 40.

tion of radical faith to an even greater extent than Israel. . . .
His confidence and his fidelity are those of a son of God — the
most descriptive term which Christians apply to him as they
contemplate their Lord."[27] In a similar vein, Ferré says that the
second of two "keys" to his book *Christ and the Christian* is
"that the historic Incarnation involves all mankind, whose
proper, potential relation to God is incarnation."[28] And, later
in the same work, he writes: "The one God is of such a nature
as to become incarnate."[29] Tillich is more traditional in his use
of the term. But this only leads him to reject the doctrine of the
Incarnation in connection with the coming of Christ as superstitious. The only possible use of the term *incarnation* is to
declare that "God is manifest in a personal life-process as a
saving participant in the human predicament."[30] That is, he allows only the generalized meaning which Niebuhr and Ferré
regard as normative. These neo-liberal views reflect the teaching of Schleiermacher accurately enough, but the latter presents
a further thought which throws his whole approach into relief.
According to Schleiermacher, every moment of the life of Christ
was "a new incarnation and incarnatedness of God, because always and everywhere all that is human in Him springs out of
that divine."[31] So incarnation was presented as the flowering of
the eternal in the temporal, whenever immanent divinity became actualized in a human subject.

It is interesting to see that belief in incarnation as a pattern
is also asserted by Van Dusen, who writes about God, the "intelligent, holy, purposeful Personality" becoming incarnate
"within the persons of men." For the immanence of God is
incarnation.

> Immanence is the presence in human spirits of some
> measure of the Divine Vision and Purity and Purpose, that
> is of the Divine Life. Complete immanence would occur

[27] *Ibid.*, p. 42.
[28] (New York: Harper Bros., 1958), p. 9.
[29] *Ibid.*, p. 191.
[30] *Systematic Theology*, II, 95.
[31] *The Christian Faith*, p. 397 (§ 96.3).

> in a genuine human person who shared, as fully as is pos-
> sible for a truly human life, the Vision and Purity and
> Purpose of God. That would be *the* Incarnation.[32]

So it appears that liberalism in the Ritschlian tradition differs
from the theology of feeling and from neo-liberalism in finding
incarnation in historical individuals rather than general human
nature or the "personal life-process." This teaching centers on
human spirits and not on the human spirit in all mankind or
in archetypal humanity.

The second assumption underlying the Christology of neo-
liberalism is that Jesus, being only one incarnation of the divine,
was not the Son of God *as Jesus* but only as overcoming the
human limitations of Jesus. Daniel Day Williams speaks about
the "discovery of positive meaning" resulting from a decision to
admit that Jesus was primarily a human "vehicle" for a revelation coming from outside himself. He asks: "Could we say
that the Christian faith claims final revelation . . . because it
gives us the picture of a finite person who acknowledges his
own limitation, and points . . . to God's truth which no finite
structure can fully express?"[33] He goes on to say that this thesis
brings about a startling reversal to traditional Christology.
But Williams does not mention the fact that Schleiermacher first
brought about this reversal. (The appeal to a "witness of
God" coming through "the limitations of existence" in Christ,
for instance, is strongly emphasized in *The Christian Faith*.)

By setting aside as outmoded the "old formulae" of the one
Person and the two natures of the Incarnate Christ, Schleiermacher introduced the fashion of speaking about the *existence*
of God *in* Christ which, naturally enough, brought about that
very division of the person of Christ which the formulae were
designed to prevent. Thus, when today Tillich protests that
Jesus Christ is not a proper name, but that we ought to use the
expression "Jesus as the Christ," he is following where Schleier-

[32] *The Vindication of Liberal Theology*, p. 139.
[33] *What Present-Day Theologians Are Thinking* (New York: Harper
Bros., 1952), p. 130.

macher led.[34] Tillich, who says that Jesus proved himself to
be the Christ by sacrificing "himself as Jesus to himself as the
Christ,"[35] takes this line of thinking to its logical conclusion.
But other neo-liberals who do not stress the point so much
accept it all the same, showing their acceptance by insisting that
Jesus only pointed men to God and is not himself to be worshipped.[36] Naturally, if Jesus is one instance of incarnation among
others, we do not have in Jesus our Emmanuel, God-with-us,
but simply one instance of Emmanuel — the chief, perhaps,
because the first. Therefore we must not worship Jesus as
the one Son of God but only insofar as we see *a* Son of God
over and above the human Jesus.

This leads to the third assumption of neo-liberal Christology.
If, as Christians we do not worship one Lord but instead
glimpse a divine Christ through the human Jesus, then revelation comes just as much from our perception of God's truth
as from Jesus' pointing to it. In the statement quoted above
concerning Jesus as a finite person, Williams says that Christian faith gives us "the picture" which points to God's truth;
and, almost at once, Williams goes on to describe how Tillich
finds the dependable core of the New Testament to be the
"picture" of Jesus given there. Once again, the inspiration
must be sought in Schleiermacher. The latter taught that the
faith in Jesus is rooted in the "impression" the disciples had of
Jesus, an impression handed down to us in the biblical "picture" of him, and not in the external events (Resurrection, Ascension, etc.) of his life.[37] This insistence upon the *picture* is
logical enough if there are continual incarnations and if Jesus
pointed beyond himself. "The uniqueness of Jesus," says Ferré,
"is the uniqueness of a historic fact, not of a relation to God

[34] *Systematic Theology*, II, 97ff.; cf. Schleiermacher, *The Christian Faith*, pp. 391ff. (§ 96.1, 2, 3).

[35] *Systematic Theology*, II, p. 123.

[36] Seè Ferré, *Christ and the Christian*, pp. 200ff., and *The Sun and the Umbrella, passim*; also Niebuhr, *Radical Monotheism*, pp. 59ff.

[37] *The Christian Faith*, pp. 418-19, 467 (§§99.1, 105.1).

inaccessible to anyone else."[38] In these circumstances, what we need is something to make historic fact live again in the present: the *picture*, in fact, which lets us see a relation of Jesus to God such that we ourselves can seek to enter into a similar relationship.[39]

The three assumptions of neo-liberal Christology actually constitute a sequence. First, it is assumed that God's sending of his Son is no unique act, but solely the first of its kind. Then it follows that the Incarnation is important in showing that God can be revealed in a human life; but the particular life is not important. So Jesus must give way to Christ in Jesus. Finally, as the *picture* of Jesus replaces the life, words, and acts of Jesus, belief in Jesus Christ, crucified and risen, is no longer held to be the distinguishing mark of Christian faith; and what is to be believed is now that deity can — and does — transform manhood into Christhood.

Christologically, neo-liberalism reproduces the teaching of Schleiermacher almost exactly. Ritschlian liberalism's defection from Schleiermacherian "orthodoxy" in this area is to be seen in its failure to adopt the second and third assumptions which I have listed. In the Ritschlian view, there was need neither for looking through the historical Jesus to discover the Christ nor for tracing a picture of Jesus as the Christ through the living consciousness of the community of belief. The meaning of Christhood was not to be sought except in the works and words of Jesus, and the "impression" of these was something we could gain straight from the record of the Synoptic Gospels. Thus Van Dusen insists strongly that Liberal Theology "affirms one person — Jesus of Nazareth and the Living Christ,

---

[38] *Christ and the Christian*, p. 213.

[39] Ferré does not ordinarily use the word "picture." But he speaks of the need for understanding the New Testament message to be "Christ as Agape, the Event-Meaning of God's Christ-deed." And he explains such an understanding as producing "a pattern of Christ, 'a picture,' as Tillich might say," (*ibid.*, pp. 55, 54). It is noteworthy that Ferré does not mention Schleiermacher's use of the picture image.

an organic unity, Jesus-Christ-in-the-life-of-the world. . . ."[40] At this point, the importance of neo-liberalism's return to Schleiermacher's "mystical" view of Christ and to an emphasis on the redemption brought by him becomes significant. The change is not absolute, but, being a revulsion from Ritschlian practicality, means that the ethical and empirical motifs recede, while the cosmic and transcendental ones shine out in the neo-liberal presentation of the meaning of faith. Such phrases as "truth and the Kingdom," "the principles and purposes of the Living God," and "what has been assumed, trusted and practised," keep recurring in Van Dusen's exposition of liberalism; and they accord well with the belief that Ritschl brought Christian faith "back to its true center."[41] In contrast with these, the typical phrases we meet with in Niebuhr, Tillich, and Ferré are "the realm of being," "the depth of reason," and "the universal truth of God as Agape." The former concern individuals in the spatio-temporal world, while the latter sink historical particularities in universal reality.

(3)

Neo-liberalism deserts the Christ of History for the Christ of Faith. But its *picture* of Jesus as the Christ is hard to reconcile with either the New Testament witness to "the Lord Jesus Christ" or the traditional creeds of Christendom. The concept of Christhood in Schleiermacher-type theology is that of adoptionism. The clearly adoptionist character of Tillich's Christology has often been noted,[42] and Ferré — whose disagreement with Tillich's outlook has been most vocal — thinks in no fashion here. A characteristic sentence of Ferré's reads: "The wonder of Christology is the mystery of the human acceptance

40 *The Vindication of Liberal Theology*, p. 89.

41 *Ibid.*, p. 186.

42 See, for example, George H. Tavard's *Paul Tillich and the Christian Message* (New York: Scribner's Sons, 1962; London: Burns & Oates), pp. 129ff. Tavard quotes other critics who have made the same diagnosis before him.

of God; on the praying Jesus comes the heavenly Dove."[43]
Nevertheless, the adoptionist note in neo-liberalism is misjudged
if it is taken simply as an indication that this is a theology which
deviates a little from tradition. The point is that neo-liberalism
has not deviated into the belief that Jesus is a Spirit-filled man.
Rather, its whole foundation demands such a belief. It knows
no other horizons than those enclosing the outlook named
Religiousness A by Kierkegaard; and Schleiermacher's preoccupation with the "vital fluidum" of man's spiritual consciousness
belongs to it as well. Therefore, when it thinks of a God-man
it thinks of a man filled by the same divine Spirit which
activates human nature generally, holding it to be axiomatic
that Christhood can be only the perfection of ordinary (natural
or not absolutely supernatural) human God-consciousness. In
this connection, we may note that Ferré says that the first
"key" to *Christ and the Christian* is that "God is not a spiritual
Personality but a personal Spirit."[44] Ferré makes the distinction,
evidently, because of liberalism's conception of God as Reality
comprehended — altogether adequately — in personal terms
(for example, Van Dusen's description of God as purposeful
Personality).[45] The neo-liberal view is that God transcends
personal categories although he is the ground and source of
the personal. Accordingly, Ferré can conceive of God as Spirit
indwelling both Jesus and mankind in what Schleiermacher
calls "the universal spiritual life."

Neo-liberal Christology actually rests, in the last resort, upon
Schleiermacher's view of universal history. For him, Christ was
one decisive stage in the unfolding of man's spirituality. The
second Adam actualized the potentialities of the first Adam.[46]
No doubt it is largely because of his reading of the story
of mankind — an essentially evolutionary reading — that
Schleiermacher's theology has appealed so strongly today. Al-

---

[43] *Christ and the Christian*, p. 249.
[44] *Ibid.*, p. 9. The second "key" has been explained above, p. 102.
[45] See above, p. 102.
[46] *The Christian Faith*, pp. 365ff., 426ff. (§ 89, 100, 106).

though the dogma of inevitable progress has proved untenable, chastened liberals are still ready to believe with Whitehead that the world which is wasting physically is also spiritually ascending.[47] Process philosophy, in fact, has been one of the influences powerfully aiding the movement back to Schleiermacher. "God's creation is His making of the world, and His leading it toward fuller, finer life," writes Williams;[48] and Ferré explains: "We are made for God and for his community. . . . Therefore God must continue his holy Incarnation to express himself and to finish in glory his own creation."[49] The theme of continuing creation in the ongoing process which brings new levels of value and meaning into human history is one blending very readily with the thought of Schleiermacher, for whom the new life produced through the influence of the Redeemer "of course presents itself as something in the process of becoming."[50]

So Richard R. Niebuhr is right in noting the central importance for Schleiermacher of his principle that in Christianity *everything* is related to the redemption accomplished by Jesus of Nazareth.[51] But Niebuhr does not go on to draw the obvious conclusion that the *kind* of redeeming activity ascribed to Jesus then controls everything. If redemption is said to be what Schleiermacher says it is, i.e., the recalling of humanity from God-forgetfulness, and the "completion of the creation of man,"[52] — then any notion that Jesus saves men from guilt and the power of sin is finally excluded. Equally, the Incarnate Christ cannot be the Man from heaven in the form of a servant. Instead, the Christ-function is to lay bare the "energy" and "potency" of God-consciousness implanted in human nature, a function that can be performed alone by some one who differs from us in

---

[47] Alfred North Whitehead, *Religion in the Making* (New York: Macmillan, 1930), p. 160. Teilhard de Chardin's writings have aroused interest once more in the evolutionary world-view.

[48] *God's Grace and Man's Hope,* p. 51.

[49] *Searchlights on Contemporary Theology,* p. 138.

[50] *The Christian Faith,* p. 476 (§ 106.1).

[51] *Schleiermacher on Christ and Religion,* p. 160.

[52] *The Christian Faith,* p. 367 (§ 89.1).

nothing except his degree of God-consciousness. Schleiermacher's God-filled man, therefore, saves men through influencing them to take their part in the completion of creation.

It is here, above all, that neo-liberalism shows itself to stand under Schleiermacher's banner. At the center of its understanding of redemption is not forgiveness of sins, but the actualizing of human potential. Criticizing neo-orthodoxy, Ferré objects: "Man is not primarily a sinner in the sight of God. He is a sinner who is basically a prodigal son. He belongs at home, if only he will come to himself, to his true self."[53] Niebuhr speaks of the Christian becoming "wholly human" through "the mediation and the pioneering faith of Jesus Christ."[54] Williams considers that we should interpret history by "what God has done in the life of Jesus to disclose the ultimate meaning of our existence," — adding, "that meaning is life in the community of love. It is the logos of our being."[55] For Tillich, salvation is first of all regeneration, or "the state of having been drawn into the new reality manifest in Jesus as the Christ," and this leads to the process of sanctification for both personality and community.[56] In other words, our faith is not in Jesus Christ the Saviour but in the Spirit which, when illustrated in the life of Jesus and conveyed to us through a continuity of consciousness, we can recognize as really ours.

The sole serious dispute among neo-liberals is concerning the cosmos which man's spiritual nature discloses and within which it develops. On one side, Tillich insists that man's spiritual awareness is of Being, so that Jesus as the Christ illustrates es-

[53] *Christ and the Christian*, pp. 104f. It is interesting to remember that both James Denney and P. T. Forsyth protested, against the liberals of their day, that the whole Christian Gospel was more than the parable of the Prodigal.

[54] *Radical Monotheism*, p. 60. Niebuhr also says that Christians are called "into membership in the society of universal being" rather than into a group with a Christ-centered faith (*ibid.*).

[55] *God's Grace and Man's Hope*, p. 79.

[56] *Systematic Theology*, II, 176ff.

sential God-manhood;[57] while, on the other side, Ferré insists that a right human perspective sees ongoing creativity, and that Jesus is the Event-Meaning disclosing Agape, the outgoing love productive of community. Both the static, ontological view and the dynamic-process view agree that Jesus manifests and expresses the reality underlying our experience of existence — a reality which, though seen most fully in Jesus, is given to us to understand by virtue of our being human. For, whatever their philosophical quarrels, neo-liberals join forces in their theological patterns of thinking. Starting with the God present in us, they find this divinity illustrated (as fully as the limits of finite existence allow) in the picture of Jesus as the archetypal man (or Christ). The picture of the Christ then awakens us to the power of the divine within us, which is our "redemption." And all of this can be found most fully in Schleiermacher.

If Schleiermacher's modern sons were to acknowledge their spiritual father without hesitation, then much confusion would be avoided. Instead of seeking an illusory middle way between liberalism and neo-orthodoxy, they could plot their progress away from the Ritschlian "heresy" and its product, Christ-of-History liberalism, back to the mainstream of Schleiermacherian "orthodoxy." Schubert M. Ogden's invoking of the broad liberal tradition, which I quoted earlier,[58] is at least a step in the right direction. For what the neo-liberals most conspicuously have in common is an outlook regarding as normative the faith in the earth-bound God revealed (as Schleiermacher explained) through human nature in universal history. They are united in rejecting the supernatural; for, even when they admit the word (as Ferré does, for example), they do not regard it as the absolutely supernatural — that which "comes down" from heaven — but merely as the unprecedented, or a leap forward in the progressive manifestation of Spirit within Nature. Similarly,

---

[57] Tillich's ontology (and the other aspects of his theology treated in this chapter) is discussed in my study, *The System and the Gospel; a Critique of Paul Tillich* (New York: Macmillan, 1963).

[58] See above, p. 41.

they find revelation to be the uncovering of the inner working of spirituality on the historical plane.[59]

To the extent to which neo-liberalism diverges from post-Ritschlian liberalism it leaves behind the latter's odd belief that, so long as we concentrate upon "practical" judgments, we can build upon a theory of reality and yet repudiate metaphysics. With Tillich and Ferré, in particular, the result has been the creation of explicit systems of philosophical theology. Yet the question arises as to whether Schleiermacher can be a guide for today. His world-view was inspired by Plato, Spinoza, Romanticism, and the atmosphere of German philosophical idealism (from which he drew and to which he contributed). And, however helped by elements from process philosophy (Ferré) or existentialism (Tillich) or other twentieth-century movements, the basis of neo-liberal thinking remains rooted in the nineteenth century. Can we take seriously into our contemporary modes of thinking an interpretation of world-history conceived in terms of the self-manifestation of Spirit?

It is not surprising, therefore, that a determined effort has been made to relate Christianity directly to modern existentialism, in order to make the Gospel meaningful in contemporary terms. This influential enterprise must now be considered.

---

[59] I have explored the anti-supernaturalistic view of revelation, with special reference to the teachings of Reinhold Niebuhr and H. Richard Niebuhr, in an article, "Revelation's Supernatural Dimension" (*The Canadian Journal of Theology*, Vol. IX, July 1963, No. 3, pp. 149-56). In the present chapter I have not discussed Reinhold Niebuhr's position among the neo-liberals, although I believe that he belongs there. His work has highly individualistic features which make direct comparison with other theologians misleading.

7

Existence Without Heaven

IS BULTMANN ALSO AMONG THE SONS OF SCHLEIER-
macher? His theological stance is sufficiently individual to require separate investigation.

There is no lack of critical estimates of Bultmann's demythologizing program, of course, and he himself has been engaged in an almost continuous dialogue with his critics. But,
since my concern is less with his individual beliefs than with
the inner logic of the demythologizing school of his creating, I
shall approach the master through one of his disciples. Schubert
M. Ogden has been introduced already as a theologian of Bultmann's Left. He stands squarely upon Bultmann's basic premise,
and, from that position, sees a need to draw conclusions more
radical than Bultmann's own theology admits.

Ogden tells us that Bultmann conceives the function of theology to be

> . . . to make explicit, in the sense of raising to conceptual
> knowledge, the understanding of human existence implicit
> in the decision of Christian faith. This means that if theo-
> logical work is properly pursued, it is neither speculative

nor scientific in an "objective" sense, but rather *existentiell*, that is, a type of thinking inseparable from one's most immediate understanding of oneself as a person.[1]

The explanation is useful for shedding light upon the word *existentiell*, but it does nothing to justify Bultmann's choice of *existentiell* understanding as a principle to be used in interpreting the Christian message. We must still ask why he thinks that this type of understanding is implicit in the decision of Christian faith. A dogma has been described. Yet we are in the dark as to why it should have been granted dogmatic status.

However, we soon learn that *existentiell* understanding is imperative, since "the theological propositions of the New Testament are not understood by modern man because they reflect a mythological picture of the world that we today cannot share."[2] By translating these propositions in terms of *existentiell* thinking we can make them meaningful for our age. For Bultmann's conviction is that the truth of the Christian message is not identical with the mythological world-view in which it was originally expressed. It was always "more" than mythological, and so it follows that New Testament myths can still be made to yield that "more," even though they now conceal rather than reveal their true message, having become obstacles to genuine faith rather than transmitters of it.

If we ask why Bultmann should have come to this conclusion, we ought to look for an answer in the dual fact that he is both a New Testament scholar and also one who has come within the orbit of Barthian theology. Previously, theologians constructing Theologies of Meaningfulness felt relatively free to handle the Gospel in the way they thought fit. Schleiermacher saw no reason why he should not begin *The Christian Faith* with propositions borrowed from ethics (in his special reading of that word), apologetics, and the philosophy of religion. Harnack, in setting forth the essence of Christianity, had no

[1] *Christ Without Myth*, p. 22.
[2] *Ibid.*, p. 24.

qualms over taking the teachings of Jesus and deducing from them certain universal truths. But now, between them, Barth and twentieth-century biblical criticism have given currency to the conviction that the Gospel is not something to be fitted into a general religious philosophy or to be identified with time-less moral principles. Instead, Christianity is constituted by the *kerygma* — a proclamation of facts concerning Jesus of Nazareth, his life, death, resurrection, and ascension. Thus, before Bult-mann can proceed to translate the Christian message into other terms, he is compelled to show that the *kerygma* is not what it has been taken to be. He has to prove that the factual references contained in the *kerygma* are largely inessential or actually misleading. The notion of myth enables him to bring forward the necessary proof, since myth is precisely the disguising of truth in pseudo-historical garb. Thus, when the kernel of the Christian message has been separated from its enveloping husk by divesting the *kerygma* of its mythological form, Bultmann believes that there will be no longer any obstacle preventing in-tellectual acceptance of Christianity by modern man.

The precise definition of myth naturally becomes very im-portant if Bultmann's demythologizing program is to be taken seriously as a reliable translation of the *kerygma*. Some critics find a certain ambiguity in Bultmann's way of identifying and describing myth. But Ogden disagrees, arguing that he holds to a concept of myth which is comprehensive and clear. He advances the following summary:

> "A mythological world-picture" is one in which (1) the non-objective reality that man experiences as the ground and limit of himself and his world is "objectified" and thus represented as but another part of the objective world; (2) the origin and goal of the world as a whole, as well as certain happenings within it, are referred to nonnatural, yet "objective" causes; (3) the resulting complex of ideas comprising the picture takes the form of a double history.[3]

[3] *Ibid.*, p. 27.

If Ogden's summary is substantially accurate (and there seems no reason to doubt it), the foundation of demythologizing theology has been declared. For, within the explanation of what is mythological, appears a statement of that reality which myth *mis*represents, namely, "the nonobjective reality that man experiences as the ground and limit of himself and his world." Here is that truth which myth presents in "unintelligible" form. The indubitable meaning of the language of the New Testament has been set forth. Through demythologization, the unbelievable world-picture of pre-scientific days has been dissolved in order to make room for the world-picture solidly established through contemporary man's self-understanding.

In short, what is most informative about the Bultmann-Ogden interpretation of myth is the information given of the underlying assumptions of the interpreters. Behind the rejection of the language of the New Testament lies an affirmation concerning ultimate reality. If this is examined, the pattern which I have noted in connection with metaphysical theologies in general becomes obvious. Ogden's three points outlaw the supernatural from the intelligible universe, from the physical universe, and from the realm of history. First, we are told that there is no reality other than man's experience of himself and his world. Second, we are not to believe that the world has a Creator or that a Providence works immanently in the world. Third, we are instructed to abandon as superstitious any reading of history which sees events in time and space as acts of God.

I have argued that metaphysical theologies begin with the assumption that the divine is immanent in man's spirit and regard transcendence solely in terms of a limit — the unconditioned ground of man's being and meaning. Ogden's claim that man experiences a "nonobjective reality" clearly belongs to this type of thinking. Reality is called "non-objective" because it does not appear within the space-time continuum but "transcends" it. Nevertheless, it is still "down here" because it is apprehended in human experience. The second characteristic of metaphysical theology to which I have referred is that it is

tied to a specific cosmology having its genesis in some particular
analysis of the structure of Being. In the case of demythologizing theology, this theoretical stiffening is provided by Heidegger.
Ogden explains that the work of interpreting the biblical myths
in terms of the *existentiell* understanding of existence is to be
carried out under the guidance of the analysis of human existence
in Heidegger's *Sein und Zeit*.[4] As I am concerned only with
the broad outlines of demythologizing theology, there is little
point in entering into the details of Heidegger's elusive thought
and complex terminology. But a word concerning the "existentialism" of *Sein und Zeit* must be said.

After considering Heidegger's theory of existence in that book,
Ogden writes:

> For man to "exist" in the technical sense that Bultmann pre-
> supposes, means he is a being who must continually face
> and answer the question of what it is to be a man. It means,
> in a word, that he is *a moral or religious being*, one who
> always has to deal with the problem of what he ought to
> be.[5]

This view of existence clarifies the meaning of faith.

> In sum, what the New Testament speaks of mythologically
> as life in faith may be appropriately translated by Heideg-
> ger's concept of "authentic" (*eigentlich*) historical existence.
> . . . If life in faith is interpreted neither as an anxious apoc-
> alypticism nor as a new supernatural state, but as an
> authentic understanding of one's existence as a person, then
> the modern man can understand the New Testament mes-
> sage.[6]

Ogden reiterates Bultmann's conviction that "the New Testament
itself both permits and requires existential interpretation."[7]
But neither part of the claim is more than questionable. The
New Testament permits this type of interpretation only if

4 *Ibid.*, pp. 44-46.
5 *Ibid.*, p. 48. Italics in the original.
6 *Ibid.*, p. 64.
7 *Ibid.*

Bultmann's view of myth is upheld and the supernatural element in the New Testament is believed to be entirely the creation of a pre-scientific world-view. And the New Testament requires this type of interpretation only if Heidegger's theory of existence is both correct and readily understood by our generation.[8]

Heidegger's teaching stands at a distance from the tradition of nineteenth-century German idealism. Yet it is remarkable how the philosophical theology constructed by the demythologizing school with his help echoes the latter. Heidegger sees man as the only sure clue to the nature of Being, and man discovers himself as he learns what it means to exist. Ogden, interpreting Heidegger, says that to discover what it means to exist is to find oneself to be a moral or religious being. Schleiermacher, classifying Christianity as belonging to the *teleological* (i.e., moral) type of religion,[9] began from the assumption that Christianity — like all religions — answered the question of what it meant to be a man. In the feeling of absolute dependence original human nature asserted itself. Where Heidegger speaks of authentic existence, Schleiermacher spoke of realizing the highest grade of human self-consciousness. Schleiermacher believed that man *ought* to become fully self-conscious, which was also to be God-conscious, since thereby he exemplified true human nature in general. Bultmann and his school believe that man *ought* to pursue *existentiell* self-understanding, since thereby he exemplifies authentic human existence. Now, Bultmann has denied that his theology can be put into the same historical line as theologies deriving from the Enlightenment, and Ogden enthusiastically supports his denial.[10] But the denial rests on the argument that *existentiell* self-understanding is not a timeless truth, such as those former theologies sought. That apology is entirely beside the point. The feeling of God-consciousness, even though it

---

[8] Paul van Buren argues that modern man does not speak Heidegger's language or find his categories meaningful. See above, p. 20.

[9] *The Christian Faith,* p. 52 (§ 11).

[10] *Christ Without Myth,* pp. 65-67.

belonged essentially to humanity, was not a general truth for
Schleiermacher. In each individual it appeared as something
that "constantly grows up and is laid hold of anew," as Bultmann says of faith as self-understanding. That is why Schleiermacher located genuine religion in feeling. No individual could
lay hold of God-consciousness by apprehending it as a timeless
reality, for it had to rise within his experience in definite "religious moments" (his term) discovered in the unfolding of historical time. Indeed, Schleiermacher's view of "piety" as the
product of the highest self-consciousness seems to be intended
to present precisely that experience indicated, in modern terminology, by "*existentiell* self-understanding."

So we must conclude that, however distant in other respects
they may be, Schleiermacher and demythologizing theologians
share a structurally identical conception of faith; and, therefore,
their approach to theology is the same. The demythologizing
theologians may protest that the faith to which they call men is
not a world-view. Nevertheless, they call men to faith of one
particular type because of the world-view which they have
adopted. They claim that they alone can guide men to the
faith which the New Testament presents in mythical form, and
they outlaw thereby every alternative interpretation of faith.
How could they object to supernaturalism's objectifying of non-
objective reality unless they had previously located non-objective
reality on their philosophical map of the cosmos? Ogden admits
as much (without drawing the plain conclusion) when he reports
on Bultmann's belief "that the conceptuality of existential philosophy provides a completely adequate vehicle for explicating the
Christian understanding of existence."[11]

If demythologizing theology adopts the same broad approach
to theology as the one taken by Schleiermacher, we may expect
to find an agreement in both outlooks over the place of Jesus
in the faith of the Christian Church. But at this point there is
division within the demythologizing camp. Ogden sums up
Bultmann's view of Christianity in two propositions:

11 *Ibid.*, p. 112.

(1) Christian faith is to be interpreted exhaustively and without remainder as man's original possibility of authentic historical (*geschichtlich*) existence as this is more or less adequately clarified and conceptualized by the appropriate philosophical analysis. (2) Christian faith is realizable, or is a "possibility in fact," because of the particular historical (*historisch*) event Jesus of Nazareth, which is the originative event of the church and its distinctive word and sacraments.[12]

Ogden points out that, if the first proposition stands, the second states too much, for "all that is required is *some* event in which God's grace becomes a concrete occurrence and is received by a decision of faith."[13] He starts his argument from Bultmann's admission that "Christian existence is nothing mysterious or supernatural," since even fallen man can have knowledge of his authentic existence.[14] Christians should not say, according to Ogden, that in Christ our salvation "becomes possible." They should say rather that in Christ what has always been possible now becomes manifest.[15]

Ogden's argument follows criticism of Bultmann on this point made in Europe by Karl Jaspers and Fritz Buri. It is an argument which chimes in with Schleiermacher's teaching. Although the latter says that Christianity is essentially distinguished from other comparable faiths "by the fact that in it everything is related to the redemption accomplished by Jesus of Nazareth,"[16] he also says that God-consciousness is always present in human nature, though it is "feeble and repressed" until "made dominant by the entrance of the living influence of Christ."[17] Since sin is primarily God-forgetfulness, man is never without some consciousness of his dependence upon God. Yet, until this consciousness is "stimulated" by the influence of the Redeemer, it

12 *Ibid.*
13 *Ibid.*, p. 123. Italics in the original.
14 *Ibid.*, p. 115.
15 *Ibid.*, p. 143.
16 *The Christian Faith,* p. 52 (§ 11).
17 *Ibid.*, p. 476 (§ 106.1).

has not power to control his life. So, what was always possible becomes manifest where the Redeemer is known. In the biblical phrase, there is a new creature — or, as Schleiermacher would paraphrase it, a new personality is in the process of becoming.

The crux of Ogden's case against Bultmann is that man's historical (*geschichtlich*) existence cannot be affected by any particular historical (*historisch*) event. Here he would have the support of Schleiermacher. For Schleiermacher as well as for Ogden there is no spiritual relevance for the believer in the confession that Jesus actually rose from the dead or ascended into heaven.[18] What matters is that there has been a decisive manifestation of human self-consciousness (and thus of God-consciousness) in Jesus of Nazareth, and that this self-consciousness is preserved in the historical (*geschichtlich*) existence of the Church. In one way, Schleiermacher is more consistent than Ogden in presenting his views, because he expounds his Christology in close relation to his philosophy of history. Jesus represents one of those sudden advances in history by means of which the progressive revelation of the character of reality as a whole is mediated. Those who come after such an advance must look back to this particular manifestation of the meaning of world-history, and so for them Jesus becomes the Redeemer. Since Ogden does not start with an explicit philosophy of history, the logic of his Christological position is not so evident. It is not clear from Ogden's presentation of demythologizing theology just how non-objective reality — the Absolute of his implicit metaphysics — comes to manifest itself in history *decisively* in Jesus of Nazareth.[19]

It is probable that Bultmann has been led into the incon-

18 *Ibid.*, 418 (§ 99.1); *Christ Without Myth*, p. 136.

19 Among modern anti-supernaturalistic theologians, Tillich comes nearest to linking Christology to a philosophy of history. He speaks of Spirit manifesting itself in history by means of revelatory *kairoi*. History, he says, is always self-transcendent but is not all of a piece. It is a "dynamic force moving through cataracts and quiet stretches" (*Systematic Theology*, III, 371). For Christians the event of Christ is "the great *kairos*." This view is very close to Schleiermacher's concept of "religious moments" in history.

sistency which his followers of the Left detect for the reason that he retains something of the Barthian view of Christ as the essential revelation of God to man. Any interpretation of Jesus of Nazareth as being in himself the Incarnate Word is obviously impossible within the perspective of a consistent demythologizing theology, for such an interpretation involves the introduction of the supernatural. And it is precisely this accusation which Jaspers, Buri, and Ogden level at Bultmann when he insists that Christian faith must remain faith in Jesus Christ as the one Lord. They point out that his belief in the absolute uniqueness of this particular historical figure involves admitting that the New Testament cannot be wholly demythologized. The view that authentic existence is made possible solely through the event of Jesus Christ assumes a "double history." The *kerygma* becomes a message *from* God *to* man (from heaven to earth) which cannot be fitted into an existentialist understanding of life.

No traces of Barthian supernaturalism, however, infect Ogden's view of Christianity. In fact, he appeals to the New Testament in order to demonstrate that faith in Jesus Christ is not the faith commended there. First, from the first chapter of Romans, he draws the conclusion that men "are utterly and radically responsible" apart from any relationship with Christ, because God has always made himself known to them and thus has "deprived them of all excuse for their self-willed estrangement from his holy presence." Second, from the fifteenth chapter of First Corinthians, he finds that the "peculiarly Christian economy of salvation has a definitely subordinate role in the ultimate outworking of God's purposes." And third, from the twenty-fifth chapter of Matthew (the parable of the Last Judgment), he has assurance that man in the New Testament is not asked essentially to have faith in Jesus Christ, but to "understand himself in the concrete situations of his existence in the authentic way that is an original possibility of his life before God."[20]

[20] *Christ Without Myth,* pp. 141-45.

Now, these conclusions present themselves, even on a cursory reading, as a very partial interpretation of their sources. St. Paul in Romans does not only underline mankind's responsibility for disregarding God's self-disclosure, but he also emphasizes the universality of the world's guilt before God. And he in no way suggests that, having failed to acknowledge God's goodness, men are to blame simply for exiling themselves from his presence. He explains that they have come under the wrath of God, so that, apart from God's decision to bring them a new chance of salvation through Christ, they are doomed. Therefore, the witness of the first chapter of Romans is that men are helpless as well as responsible. Such a conclusion Ogden — in good Pelagian fashion — finds nonsensical;[21] yet he can hardly deny that it is the clear and unavoidable teaching of St. Paul. The other two passages to which Ogden appeals are both accounts of how Jesus acts as God's vicegerent in bringing about the consummation of all things. By passing over in silence this all-important fact, Ogden misses completely the point of the passages. In connection with the account in First Corinthians, of course the work of Christ in handing over the kingdom to his Father is subordinate to his Father's purposes; for, were this not so, he would not be his Father's Son. But, equally, the Christian economy of salvation is essential to those purposes. Because Christ is God's, the purposes of God, without Christ and the salvation wrought by him, would remain unfulfilled. In the language of later Christian doctrine, the Second Person of the Trinity is neither to be confused with the First Person nor separated from the First Person. And the lesson of the parable of the Last Judgment in Matthew is that man's possibility is to serve Christ in the concrete situations of his existence, even though the true servant of his Lord will not dare believe that he has been able to rise to that supreme level of achievement. In the parable the righteous are commended because all that they did they did for Christ.

So Ogden's quotations from the New Testament support his

21 *Ibid.*, p. 118.

case only when their context is ignored and adjacent passages suppressed. Schleiermacher, with his Moravian upbringing, was better grounded in this area. Although he interpreted salvation in a non-biblical way, substituting for redemption the stimulation of undeveloped human capacity for spirituality, yet he never doubted that the hallmark of Christian faith was that it centered everything in the redemption accomplished in Jesus of Nazareth. When Ogden tries to displace from the *kerygma* the one Name which is the heart of its witness he leaves us with a New Testament unrecognizable as such. He writes that liberal theology, in trying to distinguish "the essence of Christianity" from its various historically conditioned expressions, "drew its critical standards from contemporary world-views and thus allowed modernizations of the Christian message that have been proved to be inadequate by a rigorous pursuit of its own historical method."[22] It is hard to see in what respect his own "position of the left" fails to fall under the indictment which he brings against liberalism. After all, he rejects a "mythological" presentation of the Gospel "because it is unacceptable from the standpoint of modern man's picture of himself and his world."[23]

One of Bultmann's most searching critics, Günther Bornkamm, points out that the New Testament does not merely claim for Christ that he shows us how to understand ourselves but that he takes us into a new existence which is no longer ours but his. "The new history of Christ into which I am incorporated begins and ends in heaven; in its basis and goal it radically surpasses my history and the understanding of my existence."[24] This is precisely the point. Because demythologizing theology refuses to admit a "double history" where the divine intersects with the human, it remains tied to an earthbound God who cannot lead us beyond ourselves. But the New Testament thus made

[22] *Ibid.*, p. 14.
[23] *Ibid.*, p. 137.
[24] "Myth and Gospel: A Discussion of the Problem of Demythologizing the New Testament Message," in *Kerygma and History; A Symposium of the Theology of Rudolf Bultmann*, edited by Carl E. Braaten and Roy A. Harrisville (Nashville: Abingdon Press, 1962), p. 187.

"meaningful" is not itself any longer. At best it is a new manifestation of the Testament of Human Nature, condemning man to remain in an existence without heaven. The difference between the authentic existence of demythologizing theology and eternal life is that the latter is the gift of the Lord who came down from heaven for our salvation. The New Testament presents Christ, not as a human life manifesting non-objective reality, but as an actual man who *was* the Word of God present among men. Ogden says: "The cross simply presents in a definite way the possibilities of self-understanding for which his [Christ's] entire life was the transparent means of expression."[25] But this is not the Christian message that *Christ died for us*, which is a message from "out there" and reaches us as news. The Gospel is a gospel because it is more than the confirmation of what we already know "down here."

[25] *Christ Without Myth*, p. 159.

PART THREE

The Earthbound God

2: *The Moral - Pragmatic Approach*

8

The Moral, The Numinous, and The Empirical

THOSE ANTI-SUPERNATURALISTIC THEOLOGIES
which I have named *metaphysical-mystical* had their origin in a
revulsion from natural theology, which they regarded as the offspring of an unholy alliance between rationalism and supernaturalism. Hence, from Schleiermacher down to Bultmann's
Left, we find in them a reluctance to admit to having entered
the territory of metaphysics, together with a corresponding
eagerness to claim to give merely a faithful transcript of experience. Yet the result was always to set up another type of
natural theology.[1]

The resulting "natural theology," nevertheless, was unlike
that of Thomism in two respects (as I have indicated). In the
first place — and this was the decisive break — Nature was considered to be sufficient in itself without any reference to a Supernature beyond or "over" it. So theology became a theology of

[1] This state of affairs has been noted by Thomistic thinkers, who see
in Schleiermacher's faith in the indubitability of God-consciousness a
version of the cosmological argument transposed from the external world
to the internal one. See, for example, M. C. D'Arcy, *The Nature of Belief* (London: Sheed & Ward, 1931), pp. 262f.

pure immanence in which God was simply the limit of the natural, the ground and source of all things. The earthbound God of such a theological outlook stood at the limits of experience but he was not a transcendent God in his own right. (That was why Schleiermacher outlawed from his theology the notion of the *absolutely supernatural.*) In the second place, the truths established by immanentist "natural theology" were supposed to be reached not through logical processes, but through immediate awareness. This second difference from traditional natural theology was the outcome of faith in a wholly immanent God who did not have to be deduced from the character of the world of Nature, since he was already in it and declared himself through it. In particular, this God spoke through human nature, where Nature became self-conscious. The ultimate logic of the awareness-of-God-in-humanity approach appears in the Bultmann-Heidegger theory that man does not understand himself apart from *existentiell* thinking, which is the sole route to self-understanding and so to authentic existence. But all versions of this type of theology have consistently supported some theory denying the adequacy of theory isolated from direct experience of reality (or God "down here"). On that account, the label *metaphysical-mystical* seems to be an appropriate one. In keeping with its emphasis upon the internal validation of religious truths, metaphysical-mystical theologies have from the first taken as their goal meaningfulness rather than intelligibility. Putting aside the rationalism that considers truth to be that which imprints itself on the intellect, they have set in the foreground the need of man-in-the-world to appropriate truth in the form of meaning-for-him.

Now, although metaphysical-mystical theologies were shy of bringing out into the open their metaphysical presuppositions, they did not deny them altogether. In the last resort — and sometimes before that — they were willing to defend their assumptions about the nature of reality and to argue that a particular philosophy gave support to their theological interpretations of the true meaning of the Christian faith. Whether they spoke about self-consciousness being God-consciousness, or about God as the ground of Being, or about non-objective reality as the limit of man's experience of himself and his world, they did not argue that theory was unnecessary or that a world-view was irrelevant to faith. But they did insist upon an "empirical" element (i.e., the self-revelation of immanent divinity) which was independent of any reasoning about God and which all theories concerned with religion must take into account. Schleiermacher had named the experience upon which his theology was founded "mystical" experience. However, the way was open for others to insist that the "inner experience" of the believer was an empirical fact as much as any other fact discoverable in human nature. Others, again, claimed that it was the effect of that experience, seen in the outward actions of believers, that was the true, undeniable fact. Therefore, following upon Schleiermacher's success in by-passing the entrenched positions of rationalism and orthodoxy, there developed new theological viewpoints which proceeded to justify Christianity on the grounds of its practical results. There were a variety of approaches possible along these lines. It might be argued that Jesus had lived and taught, leaving a legacy of changed lives and an influence that had permeated society and raised up a new civilization. Or it might be urged that Christian believers showed a dynamism which unbelievers could not equal. Or it might simply be said that the truth of Christianity could not be denied while there were those who were convinced, after trying the way of belief, that this "worked" for them.

These heterogeneous viewpoints may be brought together under the broad heading of the *moral-pragmatic* approach.

I have already described how Ritschlianism can be viewed, in part, as a development of what Schleiermacher spoke of as the "empirical" approach to Christ in contrast with the "mystical" approach which he himself believed to be the correct one.[2] But Ritschl derived his emphasis upon the practical element in religion (including his exclusion of metaphysics from the realm

[2] See above, pp. 87-88.

of faith and his category of the value-judgment) from Immanuel Kant.[3] The influence of Kant was so pervasive, not alone in the Ritschlian school and in post-Ritschlian liberalism but also in other varieties of religious thought through the nineteenth and early twentieth centuries, that it requires separate consideration. Like Schleiermacher, Kant did not found a school but started an era. Schleiermacher himself worked in a world that had been stirred by the consequences of Kant's "awakening from his dogmatic slumbers." Wherever the practical and the ethical side of religion was exalted, Kant was the original inspiration.

The prime importance of Kant for religious thought lies in the distinction he introduced between the spheres of the theoretical and the practical, a distinction outlined in the *Critique of Pure Reason* and taken further in the *Critique of Practical Reason*. In the Preface to his first *Critique* he explained that his intention was to deny reason in order to make way for faith. Yet the outcome of his argument was that the natural theology he excluded so rigorously from the speculative realm was brought back, in another form, and attached to the realm of morality. And so today we find that a "moral proof" of the existence of God takes its place in books on the philosophy of religion alongside other speculative proofs of deity.

That the "moral proof" is a legitimate development of Kant's postulates of pure practical reason would be somewhat hard to deny. The postulates (or presuppositions) of practical reason, according to Kant, might be acknowledged theoretically although they could not be made into the foundation for any speculative system. Nothing, in fact, forbade us to recognize

[3] Henry P. van Dusen claims that Ritschl derived his theory of value-judgments from Lotze, though he admits that Kant's agnosticism "infected his attitude, and even more that of many of his followers." (*The Vindication of Liberal Theology*, pp. 184, 35n.) But Alfred E. Garvie, while admitting that Ritschl drew his epistemology from Lotze, argues that the theory of value-judgments was taken directly from Kant. Garvie supports his argument by appealing to the pamphlet *Ueber Werthurtheile*, by Ritschl's son Otto Ritschl (*The Ritschlian Theology*, pp. 179ff.). The strongest influences upon Ritschl, says Garvie, were Kant, Schleiermacher and Lotze — in that order (*ibid.*, pp. 21f.).

what was involved in the principle of morality provided that we began from this principle and not from a "mere idea." The principle of morality itself, nevertheless, was not a postulate but a law given by the practical reason which determined the will. Now, it is not difficult for us to see here, beneath the Kantian terminology, something very much like a metaphysical theology of the Platonic-Augustinian tradition in which the primacy of the will over the intellect is asserted, and in which knowledge of God is linked to love of God. It is true that metaphysics has been expressly repudiated, and that Plato has been accused of rising on the wings of ideas into empty space. Yet these obvious differences count for very little when we note how Kant's separation of the phenomenal world, ruled by necessity, from the noumenal world of freedom corresponds to Plato's "two world" system. Furthermore, the rejection of metaphysics has come about simply because Kant considered metaphysical ideas to be no more than generalizations derived from the principles of physics, thus yielding no further truth than could be discovered in an empirical view of the universe. The Kantian vision, equally with the Platonic, sees nothing dependable in sensible appearances and seeks to penetrate to ultimate reality by means of that reason in man which is also divine. For, while Kant drew so rigid a line between speculative and practical reason, he presented both aspects of one reality; and, in the second *Critique,* he brought the two together under the guidance of practical reason. Experience of the moral demand now opened up speculative reason for practical purposes (for which end, said Kant, all theory existed) *in order that there might be no conflict in reason.*

All of which brings Kant to a genuinely Platonic position of affirming reason to be the divine principle in the universe, so that the human soul is immortal because it participates in the eternal beyond all appearances. Kant's *respect for the moral law* may seem an odd dress in which to find the Platonic Eros disguised, yet it is plain that duty in Kant's teaching is the equivalent of the Idea of the Good in Plato's, being that which both makes man what he is and also summons him to transcend his empirical self. So thoroughly does Kant's view follow the Greek "two world" system, that he refuses to admit the possibility that divinity can have anything at all to do with the world of the senses, or with human activities in space and time.

> Consequently, if I say of beings in the world of sense that they are created, I regard them only as noumena. Just as it would therefore be contradictory to say God is the creator of appearances, it is also a contradiction to say that He, as the Creator, is the cause of actions in the world of sense, as these are appearances; yet at the same time He is the cause of the existence of the acting beings (as noumena).[4]

Those who champion the Platonic-Augustinian tradition of metaphysical theology find in Kant an ally, since his anti-speculative stand opposes Thomistic natural theology (which is prepared to argue directly from our recognition of the world of contingent being to necessary Being, i.e., *the* necessary Being, God), while it supports a "mystical" theology declaring the human spirit to be immediately aware of the divine immanent in its sense of absolute moral obligation. According to Tillich, for example, the lesson of the categorical imperative is the indubitable force of man's experience of the unconditional element in himself and his world.[5] And it would seem that the same lesson is taught even more clearly in Kant's confession of his feelings in contemplating the starry heavens above and the moral law within. In this confession we can see that to attribute to Kant a mystical outlook — on the fact of it, an unlikely imputation — is, after all, appropriate. Here experience of the unconditional meant for Kant an intimation of a reality which transcended alike his individuality (the starry heavens were

---

[4] *Critique of Practical Reason and Other Writings in Moral Philosophy*, ed. Lewis White Beck (Chicago: University of Chicago Press, 1949), pp. 207f.

[5] *Systematic Theology*, I, 206. Tillich points out that Kant is not justified in proceeding, on this basis, to God as an unconditioned Being, the supreme Lawgiver (*ibid.*, p. 207).

impersonal) and his reasoning powers (the moral law was not invented by merely taking thought) and yet which lived in his individual mind. As he himself said of those "two things" which "fill the mind with ever new and increasing wonder and awe" —

> I do not merely conjecture them and seek them as though obscured in darkness or in the transcendent region beyond my horizon: I see them before me, and I associate them directly with the consciousness of my own existence.[6]

The inference must be, as Tillich holds, that man and his world are self-transcending; or, in Ogden's terms, that man experiences non-objective reality as the ground and limit of himself and his world. And Kant's teaching confirms this. For him the moral law did not come to us from "out there" beyond ourselves. It was the law of *our own nature* as noumenal beings; it was self-legislation. God, as a postulate of the practical reason was only to be presupposed because the self required a *summum bonum* to relate itself to in order to know itself to be part of a teleological order. And, as such a complex presupposition could not be wholly convincing, Kant's final conclusion in his *Opus Postumum* was that God was the moral law itself. Here the God who was Providence gave place, logically enough, to the God who was a cosmic principle; and so even a formal theism disappeared in a pure immanence.

If Kant's teaching belongs, at a remove, to the Platonic-Augustinian tradition of metaphysical theology,[7] with his concept of practical reason following the metaphysical-mystical approach to the earthbound God, it remains to be shown why his influence was so potent a force in creating the moral-pragmatic approach. As I have already indicated (and illustrated in connection with Ritschl) the latter approach was necessarily rooted in the former and dependent upon it. Kant did not change the basis of the

---

[6] Conclusion to the *Critique of Practical Reason* (*op. cit.*, p. 258).

[7] An interesting comparison might be made between Kant's division between speculative and practical reason and St. Augustine's division between *scientia* and *sapientia*. While the contrasted terms are not equivalents, of course, there are evident points of contact linking them.

theology of immanence and belief in the divinity revealing itself
in human nature as such. But, if nothing had been changed,
at least something had been challenged, although Kant's denying of (one sort of) reason in order to make room for (rational)
faith was a robbing of Peter to pay Paul; and it left reason in
its comprehensive sense the authoritative source of religion.
Nevertheless the term *metaphysics* had been down-graded and
speculation had been given a bad name. At the same time, religion had been linked conspicuously with morality.

Pure moral law, Kant insisted, must be a form without content, open to the universal which is reason's domain. But the
most obvious thing about morality is that it is concerned with
particular events and cannot be conceived in wholly universal
fashion without becoming a shadow of itself. So, while Kant
shunned the merely empirical, the result of his talk about the
primacy of practical reason was, in the long run, to exalt the
notion of practical moral action in the ethical sphere. Moreover, moral experience is not only bound up with particular
acts; for it also involves us with other individuals. Here we
are not likely to remain content with the Kantian formula that
every person is an end and not a means. In ordinary terms, to
treat a person as an end in himself means, in the first place, not
to put him into a class, and therefore not to regard him as an
example of human nature as such — a noumenal self to be ap-
rehended through a phenomenal envelope. By stressing the
bond between morality and religion, Kant actually helped to
break down the barrier he had erected between the noumenal
and the phenomenal. He brought the Enlightenment, which
viewed individuals as reflections of man's general nature, into
proximity with Romanticism, which viewed each individual as
a unique expression of the infinite variety of Nature. (In this
connection, Kant's unbounded admiration for Rousseau's writings is of more than casual interest.) And although his *Religion Within the Limits of Reason Alone*, with its presentation of Jesus in terms of a life in perfect obedience to the moral
law, was highly rationalistic, yet it encouraged the belief that

the essence of Christianity consisted in high ethical precept and performance.

With Ritschl and the emphasis upon the Kingdom of God interpreted as "the organization of humanity through action inspired by love," the shift from practical reason eschewing the empirical to practical religion involved in the empirical had declared itself. Ritschl, nevertheless, thought of his teaching as being in line with the theology of the Reformation and so kept a place, even if an inadequate one, for individual redemption. The next chapter examines some of the forms of Christianity proposed by thinkers who believed that a practical, empirical, and ethical faith *contained* all the redemption required.

There remains another religious approach, however, which owes much to Kant and yet which does not accent the moral dimension of Christianity. This is the approach which follows Kant in believing that faith must be discovered in the practical reason, but proposes another non-speculative source for knowledge than that of the moral law. In this area, the thinker most plainly indebted to Kant is Rudolf Otto.

In *The Idea of the Holy* Otto wrote that the "holy" or numinous consciousness is a *purely a priori* category, pointing to

> . . . a hidden substantive source, from which the religious ideas and feelings are formed, which lies in the mind independently of sense-experience; a 'pure reason' in the profoundest sense, which because of the surpassingness of its content, must be distinguished from both the pure theoretical and the pure practical reason of Kant, as something yet higher or deeper than they.[8]

He criticized Schleiermacher for restricting his feeling of absolute dependence to *self*-consciousness, with the result that God was brought in subsequently merely as the cause required to account for an existing effect. Such a procedure involved an

[8] *The Idea of the Holy; an Inquiry into the Non-Rational Factor in the Idea of the Divine and its Relation to the Rational* (Eng. trans., London: Oxford Univ. Press, 1924), p. 118.

appeal to rationalistic thinking quite out of keeping with
a starting-point in religious emotion. He himself wished to
keep to non-rational ground entirely, but equally to avoid
being imprisoned within subjectivity; and he thought that the
category of the holy established all that was needful in that
direction. The numinous was an actual experience, not a rational
abstraction. And it could be known directly, through a *numen
praesens* or the holy as a reality entering into our consciousness.
The numinous was always "felt as objective and outside the
self."[9]

Fundamentally, Otto has not moved off the Schleiermacherian
platform. He merely gives us a slightly different analysis of
religious self-consciousness from Schleiermacher's. Certainly, he
is no more "objective" than Schleiermacher, for why should that
which is *felt* as objective *be* objective? He appeals continually
to the irreducibly mystical nature of religion, and insists that
its character is to be redemptive so that his approach conforms
very closely indeed to the metaphysical-mystical type. We are
back on the familiar track of the divine as immanent in man
and revealed through a state of awareness (called by Otto
the faculty of divination),[10] the rejection of supernaturalism,[11]
the work of Jesus viewed through the "picture" of his person
and life,[12] and the belief that the true nature of man is only
gradually made manifest in history.[13] What sets Otto apart
from Schleiermacher, however, is not the content of his teaching but the spirit of it. While he still depends upon the pre-

9 *Ibid.*, p. 11.
10 *Ibid.*, p. 148.
11 *Ibid.*, pp. 148f.
12 *Ibid.*, p. 172.
13 *Ibid.*, pp. 179-82. Otto claimed that the distinction between the
category of the holy and "holiness as revealed in outward appearance"
corresponded to the distinction between reason (in the sense of all cognition arising "in the mind from principles native to it") and history. All
were capable of having *a priori* cognitions, but first had to be "awakened"
through the mediation of "highly endowed natures." Here the parallel
with Schleiermacher's view of God-consciousness in human nature and in
history is complete.

supposition of a world-history disclosing the really real through surface appearances, he writes as though the surface appearances were his chief concern. He documents his study of the holy by multiplying references to the data of comparative religion, giving the impression that essential human nature can be identified by accumulating a large number of facts drawn from the empirical order. He shows little sign of sharing Schleiermacher's view that the seat of religious awareness is in human nature in general and not in individuals inhabiting the "sensuous" order (and no more of appreciating Kant's restriction of practical reason to the noumenal aspect of acting beings). Tillich, indeed, makes a Schleiermacherian judgment upon *The Idea of the Holy* when he says that it is phenomenological analysis describing indirectly and "beyond Otto's own intention" the experience of ultimate reality as the ground of man's being.[14] It seems that Otto considers that his category of the holy is proved in history, in spite of his admission that "Religion is only the offspring of history so far as history on the one hand develops our disposition for knowing the holy, and on the other is itself repeatedly the manifestation of the holy."[15]

The *Idea of the Holy* shows us the genesis of an attempt to demonstrate that a theology based on "religious experience" need not depend on a metaphysical world-view but can pass directly to an appeal to empirically grounded facts. Such an attempt is self-defeating, because the "facts" appealed to are not bare facts of the kind which an empiricist would admit; for they are already interpreted as *meaningful* within a universe understood as the realm where the divine becomes evident in the human — man's spirit being progressively aware of Spirit. Be that as it may, in Otto's day and later there were a number of theologians who made the attempt to prove the objectivity of religious faith on the basis of the subjective reception of religious "reality," arguing that there was sufficient empirical

[14] *Systematic Theology*, I, 215f.
[15] *The Idea of the Holy*, p. 181.

evidence to establish the truth of the basic claims of Christianity. Among these were D. C. Macintosh and Henry Nelson Wieman.

D.C. Macintosh developed his opinions apart from Otto, and his references to that thinker were always less than enthusiastic.[16] He was carried along in the Ritschlian current of practicality, conceiving Christology to consist in a right assessment of the "permanent contributions of the historic Jesus to humanity."[17] But he also believed that the time had come to reconsider Ritschl's anti-metaphysical bias. So he declared his intention to be that of reconciling the Ritschlian and the Hegelian traditions on the basis of the proposition that "the spiritually valuable content of historic Christianity is true."[18] His belief that theology could be both empirical and scientific was summed up in the short and simple argument that "Revelation of the reality of God in the religious experience of moral salvation is as normal and natural as any other process of cognition. It is the discovery of reality through experience."[19] The God of "experimental religion" was also an "existent Factor" guaranteeing "dependable religious experience," and thus "universally verifiable."[20]

The most prominent feature of Macintosh's empirical theology is that it does not put all its confidence in empiricism, but appeals openly for additional support. Macintosh explained that his type of empirical theology needed to be supplemented

[16] Macintosh presented a paper, "Theology as an Empirical Science," to the American Theological Society in 1914, three years before Otto's book appeared in Germany, and his book on the subject (carrying the same title as his paper) was published in 1919.   See Douglas Clyde Macintosh, *The Problem of Religious Knowledge* (New York: Harper & Bros., 1940), p. 190. His view of Otto was that the Kantian framework of his thought prevented him from acknowledging direct religious perception, even though his concept of *divination* gave the impression that he did, and that he never went beyond Schleiermacher's preoccupation with the feeling-side of religious experience (*op. cit.*, pp. 297-303).

[17] *The Reasonableness of Christianity* (New York: Scribner Press, 1925, 1926), p. 149.

[18] *Ibid.*, p. 16.

[19] *Ibid.*, p. 126.

[20] *Ibid.*, p. 127.

both by a "normative theology of religious intuition or faith" and by a "reasonably tenable metaphysical theology."[21] And it would seem to be evident that any program seeking to reconcile Ritschlianism and Hegelianism must actually assume from the first a harmony of the three sorts of theology. At any rate, Macintosh insisted that he found it absolutely necessary to adopt a monistic epistemology, which he called *critical realism*. He argued that science and philosophy equally had their source in critical common sense, and that a critical monistic realism was the logical theoretical elaboration of the common sense view.[22] Kantian dualism, forcing a separation between the realms of the phenomenal and the noumenal, was in his eyes the chief obstacle to the acceptance of a genuinely empirical theology. For this reason, Otto had been unable to escape from a limiting subjectivity, while he himself had been able to show that the evidence of experimental religion demanded recognition of the existent Factor, God.

In his later expositions of empirical theology, Macintosh freely admitted that his general approach had much in common with the theology of Henry Nelson Wieman.[23] And he found it possible to incorporate "the essential of Wieman's definition" of God, along with his own.[24] While he championed *the new Christian supernaturalism* (as he termed it), Wieman stood for what he called *the newer naturalism*. Evidently the two world-views were not essentially different.

Throughout his long career, Wieman has shown a remarkable consistency of outlook in advocating a naturalism that finds room for religious faith. Naturalism, as he sees it, stands firmly on the claim that "all knowledge of actualities must be gained

[21] *The Problem of Religious Knowledge* (Chapters 20 "Normative Theology," 21 "Metaphysical Theology"), pp. 357-382, especially pp. 306, 373. See also *The Reasonableness of Christianity* (Chapters 11 "Knowledge in General," 12 "Religious Knowledge," 13 "Reality"), pp. 161-281.
[22] *The Reasonableness of Christianity*, pp. 163, 209.
[23] *The Problem of Religious Knowledge*, p. 165.
[24] *Ibid.*, p. 173.

by empirical methods requiring observation of predicted consequences."[25] On these grounds he is convinced that the reality of God is assured.

> Whatever else the word God may mean, it is a term used to designate that Something upon which human life is most dependent for its security, welfare and increasing abundance. That there is such a Something cannot be doubted. The mere fact that human life happens, and continues to happen, proves that this Something, however unknown, does certainly exist.[26]

Process philosophy has provided him with the categories by means of which he has described the universe. Taking his cue from A. N. Whitehead (with some additional prompting by Henri Bergson), he finds creation permeated by creative energy which, working against obstacles, brings about ever higher levels of creative good. Thus we are all searching for God, and achieving the fulfillment of life insofar as we discover him. As against the naturalism of John Dewey, who would not admit the religious element in life except as interpreted in terms of human imagination, Wieman insists that there is "a creativity working antecedently to the mind, creating it along with its world."[27] Here again, his position merges with that of Macintosh, who argued that Dewey's form of empiricism was the offspring of psychological idealism and therefore unduly subjectivistic, since it disregarded the empirical evidence that religious faith did have objective effects.[28]

Wieman's support of Christianity is also very close to Macintosh's valuation of Christian faith in terms of the permanent contribution of the historic Jesus to humanity. According to Wieman, Jesus was experimenting. "He was testing a proposi-

[25] *A Handbook of Christian Theology* (New York: Meridian Books, The World Publishing Co., 1958), article "Naturalism," p. 243.

[26] *Religious Experience and Scientific Method* (New York: Macmillan, 1926), p. 9.

[27] *The Source of Human Good* (Chicago: Univ. of Chicago Press, 1946), pp. 194-195.

[28] *Op. cit.*, pp. 82f., 95-96, 197.

tion in order to make manifest and pervasive throughout human living that behavior of the universe which is God."[29] He attempted to live a life of creative love. Therefore, that creative energy which always and everywhere creates further good was manifest in Jesus. It was seen in him because he existed in it. The fellowship which he founded felt it. "Thus each was transformed, lifted to a higher level of human fulfilment."[30] After the resurrection, the experiment of Jesus bore fruit, and the transforming power previously known only where he was present now spread through all the world. "But what rose from the dead was not the man Jesus; it was creative power. . . . It was Christ the God, not Jesus the man."[31]

We are back once more with the familiar division between the human Jesus and the Christ manifest in him through the Spirit immanent in man's spirit.[32] So, in the end, it seems that whether we tread in the steps of Schleiermacher and find divinity within self-consciousness, or whether we follow the empirical theologians and trace divinity in the external manifestations of religion, this makes very little difference to the reading of Christianity which results. The new Christian supernaturalism and the newer naturalism alike stay within the boundaries fixed by Schleiermacher's rejection of the absolutely supernatural. Empirical theology reveals itself as one more version of the theology of immanence. What is special about it is that it has chosen to see the divine in the outward effects of the spiritual life of humanity instead of in the inward springs of that life. Schleiermacher said that in the "redemption" realized for humanity in Christ mankind is conscious of its real nature. Macintosh and Wieman reply that, in that same divine-human event,

---

[29] *The Wrestle of Religion with Truth* (New York: Macmillan, 1927), p. 67.

[30] *The Source of Human Good,* p. 40.

[31] *Ibid.,* p. 44.

[32] The tendency found in Schleiermacherian theology to make God wholly a pervasive Spirit is seen in Wieman's identification of God with creative power. Macintosh also finds that "divinely functioning reality" is just the Holy Spirit (*op. cit.,* p. 360).

mankind achieves its true purpose and can point to its actual accomplishments. Yet the evidence appealed to is substantially the same: the actualization of human potentialities in history.

Macintosh and Wieman both believed in a God, a Something invisibly present in the world as a spiritual force directing it. There have been other attempts to advocate religious faith on empirical grounds without taking this course, at least, not openly. These have not argued only that theology deals with the facts of human experience but also that we can support the essence of Christianity without being involved in positing any non-objective or trans-empirical reality. Theologies of this more radically pragmatic and empirical kind are my concern in the next chapter.

9

Religion Without Theology and Theology Without God

ONE OF THE MOST CONSISTENT AND STRENUOUS opponents of supernaturalism was John Dewey, whose *A Common Faith* proposed an empirical faith which would be the negation of religion and yet preserve all the human values previously found in man's religious attitudes and activities. *A Common Faith* referred briefly to the changes evident in the religious outlook since the Middle Ages. The Renaissance showed a new birth of secularism, while the eighteenth century introduced the idea of "natural religion," largely in protest against the dominance of ecclesiastical power.

But natural religion no more denied the intellectual validity of supernatural ideas than did the growth of independent congregations. It attempted rather to justify theism and immortality on the basis of the natural reason of the individual. The transcendentalism of the nineteenth century was a further move in the same general direction, a movement in which "reason" took on a more romantic, more color-

143

ful, and more collective form. It asserted the diffusion of the supernatural through secular life.[1]

Dewey was confident that he had broken completely with transcendentalism because he had divorced "mystical" experience from the supernatural. His formula for a common faith was purely humanistic and this-worldly. It required no vision of a reality beyond the actual, scientifically guaranteed world of the senses. It required no God, whether declared by revelation in some sacred writings or discovered by supersensuous awareness in the depth of the human spirit. It retained the word *God* simply as a courtesy title, permitted because men commonly preserve familiar forms of speech to express new concepts. And it declared the need to kill religion in order to free *the religious,* i.e., human ideals promoting the good life. Those ideals, formerly projected upon a non-actual divine Being, were now to be collectively put to work as "the unity of loyalty and effort evoked by the fact that many ends are one in the power of their ideal, or imaginative, quality to stir and hold us."[2]

Dewey's declared purpose was to abolish the last vestiges of nineteenth-century transcendentalism and to establish a purely naturalistic reading of man's religious behavior (and no nonsense about any *newer naturalism,* either!) Yet it may be doubted whether he entirely succeeded. What he denied was plain enough. God immanent as well as God transcendent had to be displaced. Preachers of supernaturalism, of natural religion, and of the experience of the divine were alike deluded. On the other side, what he asserted was less plain. John Macquarrie has commented that, since the religious attitude which Dewey supported was so different from the ordinary

[1] *A Common Faith* (New Haven: Yale Univ. Press, 1934), pp. 64f. Dewey speaks of the "diffusion of the supernatural" where I have spoken of "an earthbound God." He would regard any concept of "spirit" or "nonobjective reality" as still within the supernaturalistic circle of ideas. With this difference, his account of nineteenth-century transcendentalist religious thought supports my own.

[2] *Ibid.,* p. 43.

understanding of religion, it is hard to see why he should want to go on talking about religion at all.[3] This is the question which demands an answer. The answer may very well be that he wished to claim for his vision of "the common faith of mankind" the same kind of finality that religious faiths have always had for the faithful. He felt that something as intangible as an ideal was nevertheless completely *real*, and that to believe fervently in such a reality was the sole hope for mankind.

Yet, in putting his trust thus in what has since been termed "nonobjective reality," Dewey had surely fallen back upon a version of that nineteenth-century transcendentalism which he had thought to leave behind, and had admitted an immanent God. He wrote: "An ideal is not an illusion because imagination is the organ through which it is apprehended."[4] But what special reality did he attribute to that which was apprehended through this "organ", so that he could be certain it was no illusion? Even though his explicit stand was upon the "natural facts" established by means of the experimental sciences, he appealed implicitly to a realm beyond those facts. His faith in the power of ideals pointed to a hidden metaphysic, to belief in a universe so constituted that it permitted the actualizing of ideals and thus was, in some sense, the abode of Spirit. Hence the criticisms of Wieman and Macintosh[5] were not without foundation. Dewey's exposition of his faith in the power of ideals lacked final coherence apart from the supposition of an immanent deity manifesting himself within the world-process.

Thus, in spite of appearances, Dewey's spiritual kinship must be judged to be with the transcendentalists. He said that the latter stood for the diffusion of the supernatural through the secular. If we understand *supernatural* here to mean *transcendent* (as we must, for they were anti-supernaturalists to a man), the same is true of the teaching of *A Common Faith*.

[3] *Twentieth-Century Religious Thought; the Frontiers of Philosophy and Theology, 1900-1960* (New York: Harper & Row, 1963), p. 180.

[4] *A Common Faith*, p. 43.

[5] See above, p. 140.

Dewey simply wished to diffuse the transcendent in the secular without remainder. To use Tillich's terminology, he wished to retain the dimension of depth in human experience without acknowledging any Ground of being. It is instructive to observe how close his program for a faith in ideals comes to Schleiermacher's view of piety as a feeling of absolute dependence. Indeed, when he described the benefits to be derived from a right exercise of the "religious function," he pressed into service language similar to that used by Schleiermacher to explain the meaning of redemption. A religious attitude, he urged, will not deal with man in isolation, as supernaturalism does, for it "needs the sense of a connection of man, in the way of both dependence and support, with the enveloping world that the imagination feels is a universe."[6] A. M. Fairbairn's summary of Schleiermacher's teaching, quoted earlier, might apply equally well, on another level, to Dewey:

> He took his stand on religion, and saved it from friends and enemies alike. He resolved it into a thing essentially human, necessary to man. . . . But the feeling, as it was of dependence, could not live in isolation; the universe was in ceaseless activity, revealing itself to us and in us every moment; and to be moved by what we thus experienced and felt, not as separate units, but as parts of a whole, conditioned and supplemented by all the rest, was religion.[7]

Nevertheless, Dewey did not become another Schleiermacher; nor did he, like Schleiermacher's modern sons, construct a philosophical theology. He was not interested in theology but in morality. Admitting mystical experience, he was still afraid that mysticism might lead to a retreat from the world instead of a determination to change it for the better. He insisted, therefore, that the religious attitude was one discovering the union of man with "God" through uniting actual conditions with ideal ends. It was "natural and moral," "active and practical."

6 *Ibid.*, p. 53.
7 See above, pp. 69-70.

It selected "those factors in existence that generate and support our ideas of good as an end to be striven for."[8]

By taking this stand, Dewey illustrates for us the distinctive mark of the pragmatic approach to religion. Such an approach cannot avoid raising theological issues, but it regards theology as such to be a profitless occupation. It analyzes the meaning of religion only up to the point where it can be shown to be real enough to be of service. Beyond that point it does not wish to go. The religious pragmatist applies to theologians the comment of Karl Marx about philosophers: they had explained the world in various ways, and the task remained to change it. All the same, the pragmatist may be over-eager to move from theoretical analysis to practical application; and, oddly enough, this over-eagerness often shows itself in an excessively theoretical approach, overlooking the realities of the situation. Dewey illustrates this aspect of pragmatism also. He seemed to think that it was enough to announce the death of supernaturalism, argue that the springs of religious faith were immanent in man, and then appeal to the world to drop all religions and adopt the religious attitude as outlined by him. A Common Faith ended with the words: "Such a faith has always been implicitly the common faith of mankind. It remains to make it explicit and militant."[9] We might add that such a faith is religiously anemic. A militant Church of the Common Faith could never arise on the foundation of Dewey's abstract creed and undeveloped theology.

Behind Dewey's pragmatic justification of the religious attitude stands the pragmatism of William James. His belief in man's discovery of his unity with "the enveloping world" through imagination has its roots in James's presentation of religious experience as awareness of the subconscious continuation of our conscious life.

> Disregarding the overbeliefs, and confining ourselves to what is common and generic, we have in *the fact that the*

[8] *A Common Faith,* pp. 52, 53.
[9] *Ibid.,* p. 87.

> *conscious person is continuous with a wider self through which saving experiences come,* a positive content of religious experience which, it seems to me, *is literally and objectively true as far as it goes.*[10]

So much James thought to be empirically given. Going on from there to give his own "overbelief" (or creative interpretation of the facts), James identified the wider self with which our subconscious self connected us with a higher part of the universe. This was located in "an altogether other dimension of existence" from the sensible world, in a "mystical" or "supernatural region" where our ideals resided. "God is the natural appellation, for us Christians at least, for the supreme reality, so I will call this higher part of the universe by the name of God. . . . God is real since he produces real effects."[11] So James concluded that religious experience did guarantee God, so long as there was no attempt to demand that this deity should conform to the standards of supernaturalistic orthodoxy.

Here we have an empirical approach to religion which shows its affinity with transcendentalism more openly than does Dewey's "common faith." Etienne Gilson has commented: "After reading W. James, I still want to know if my religious experience is an experience of God, or an experience of myself."[12] But the answer is, surely, "Both!" What James says about God is said about us also, to the extent to which we participate in God through our continuity with the wider self. For we do not inhabit simply the sensible world. On another level, within the "mystical" region, we are what God is. There is a striking similarity between James's distinction between the *conscious self* and the *wider self* and Schleiermacher's distinction between the *sensible self-consciousness* and the *highest self-consciousness*. From his own point of view, James would

---

[10] *The Varieties of Religious Experience, A Study in Human Nature* (New York: Longmans, Green, 2nd edition, 1902), p. 515. (Italics in the original.)

[11] *Ibid.*, pp. 156, 517.

[12] *Reason and Revelation in the Middle Ages* (New York: Scribner's Sons, 1938), p. 97.

have agreed with Schleiermacher's dictum that, for the man who recognizes what piety is, "every moment of a merely sensible self-consciousness is a defective and imperfect state."[13] And he never tired of arguing that no dogmatic opinion (such as scientific positivism) should be allowed to veto the response of the self to the call of the ideal in religious faith.[14]

Of course, James's point of view was moral-pragmatic and not mystical-metaphysical. The author of *A Pluralistic Universe*[15] could not have assented to the monistic conclusions reached by Schleiermacher concerning the Whence of our highest self-consciousness. At the same time, true to his pragmatic principles, he did not try to disprove the transcendental world-view. Instead, he maintained that religions (as distinct from theologies) have always been polytheistic, and that it was reasonable, therefore, to think that our union with a higher reality discovered in religious experience might be union with one power out of many.[16] Such a pluralism left room for risk and genuine moral effort, since transcendental absolutism ruled out individual intitiative by suggesting that all things took their appointed places within the Whole. At the other extreme, crude naturalism was a creed for radically tough-minded presons feeling not the least need for religion. He concluded that, for those among his readers who were neither over-tough nor over-tender, "the type of pluralistic and moralistic religion that I have offered is as good a religious synthesis as you are likely to find."[17]

James's brand of religion, in the end, demands a universe made up to the prescription of a pragmatist of a moralistic turn of mind; and, if we do not care to accept what he has offered, this

---

[13] *The Christian Faith*, p. 22 (§5.3).
[14] See especially "Is Life Worth Living?" in *The Will To Believe and Other Essays in Popular Philosophy* (New York: Longmans, Green, 1897).
[15] New York: Longmans, Green, 1909.
[16] *The Varieties of Religious Experience*, pp. 524-527; *Pragmatism*, p. 298.
[17] *Pragmatism*, p. 301.

may be because we are pragmatists of a different sort. (A
painter or poet, for instance, might be a pragmatist, and yet
see no need for a moralistic religion. His would be a will to
believe in a universe permitting and advancing aesthetic harmony, so that he might be inclined to turn away from pluralism
also.) Alternatively, we may reject James's offer because we
do not think that we are free to prescribe what the universe shall
be simply because a certain constitution of reality would justify
our present attitudes and strivings. In short, we may repudiate
the pragmatic attitude *in toto*. In this event, we are likely to
agree with Josiah Royce, who wrote in his essay on "William
James and the Philosophy of Life" that his friend's philosophy
of religion, as it stood, was chaotic.[18] Royce discovered in
James's actual ethical judgments "the repeated recognition of
certain essentially absolute truths" which showed him to have
absorbed much of the ethical idealism of Fichte. He "was in
spirit an ethical idealist to the core," and far nearer to Hegel
than he supposed.[19]

Behind pragmatism looms the shadow of transcendentalism.
And, if pragmatists fail to recognize this, it is because they
have decided not to look around.

Yet, for a time, it seemed to many that pragmatism offered
the best hope for religious faith, finding room for belief in an
age dominated by an increasingly vocal scientific positivism
and an increasingly persuasive secularism. Parallel with the
pragmatism of William James was the intuitionism of Henri
Bergson;[20] and the pragmatic approach dominated also the
Catholic Modernist movement of the early years of the present
century.[21] A previous form of pragmatism, however, was even
more influential in its day and has been taken up again quite
recently: the religious teaching of Matthew Arnold.

18 *William James and Other Essays on the Philosophy of Life* (New
York: Macmillan, 1911), p. 25.
19 *Ibid.*, pp. 42-43. This judgment could be applied also to Dewey.
20 See Gilson, *op. cit.*, pp. 96-98.
21 See Macquarrie, *op. cit.*, pp. 181-186. Macquarrie's whole chapter
"Pragmatism and Allied Views" (pp. 169-193) is of great interest.

Arnold's *St. Paul and Protestantism* was published first in 1869 and was followed by *Literature and Dogma* in 1873. With the exception of Feuerbach (whose *Essence of Christianity* had been translated by George Eliot in 1854), Arnold was the first thinker to submit the Bible to what we now think of as demythologization. "The object of *Literature and Dogma*," he wrote in his Preface to the popular edition of that work, "is to re-assure those who feel attachment to Christianity, to the Bible, but who recognise the growing discredit befalling miracles and the supernatural."[22] Christianity could continue to stand only by its *natural truth.* "It is after this that, among the more serious races of the world, the hearts of men are really feeling; and what really furthers them is to establish it."[23] And so he proposed to establish the natural truth of the Bible upon a verifiable basis in place of the unverifiable assumptions of the theology of the Christian churches. He accepted the task of separating the essence of Christianity from the theological frame in which it had been set heretofore. "Christianity is immortal; it has eternal truth, inexhaustible value, a boundless future."[24]

In *St. Paul and Protestantism* Arnold argued that the Apostle was, although a mystic, a moralist first and last. In *Literature and Dogma* he explained that the whole sweep of biblical religion, from the Old Testament to the New, was a concern with conduct. Jesus went beyond the finest ethical teaching of the prophets, because he had a new and different way of putting things. When he spoke, his hearers both knew the difference between ceremony and conduct and saw "by a flash the true reason of things." He made them feel "that they had a best and real self as opposed to their ordinary and apparent one, and that their happiness depended on saving this best self from being overborne."[25] But, alas, human

---

[22] *Literature & Dogma; an Essay Towards a Better Apprehension of the Bible* (London: Smith, Elder, 1895), vii. This Preface was written in 1883.

[23] *Ibid.,* ix.

[24] *Ibid.,* xii.

[25] *Ibid.,* p. 67.

beings have never been able to stay with beliefs which are
natural and verifiable. "That the spirit of man should entertain
hopes and anticipations, beyond what it actually knows and can
verify, is quite natural."[26] Hence extra-belief — *Aberglaube*
— enters the picture. In itself harmless and inspiring (Goethe:
der Aberglaube ist die Poesie des Lebens), extra-belief becomes hardened into dogma and so into pseudo-science which
degenerates into superstition. The Old Testament expectation
of a Messiah gives birth to the miraculous story of the pre-ex-
istent Son of God. Jesus becomes the Second Person of the
Trinity, and the result is the Catholic doctrine of the Mass and
the Protestant doctrine of Justification. And now *the masses*
are losing the Bible and its religion. Such was the account
which Arnold gave of the history of Christianity. The original
essence of biblical religion had almost been lost, thanks largely
to the misguided toil of theologians. The Athanasian creed, for
example, was a grotesque mixture "of learned pseudo-science
with popular *Aberglaube*."[27]

Arnold was able to advance an early form of demythologizing
program because of his competence in literary criticism. His
Literature and Dogma suggested that the Bible must necessarily
be misinterpreted if its readers were unacquainted with the
nature of literature — which, moreover, was the true key to
life and the spirit of man. The prime error of the theologians
was that they confused poetry with science. The Bible, rightly
understood, was needful for "the right inculcation of righteousness" and, more particularly, "for the right inculcation of the
method and secret of Jesus" which was *epieikeia,* the temper
of sweet reasonableness.[28] And to read the Bible aright and to
profit from our reading was "an experimental process," one which
would establish the fundamental truth of religion — its natural
truth — *the necessity of righteousness.*[29] Here we can see, in

26 *Ibid.,* p. 58.
27 *Literature and Dogma,* p. 159.
28 *Ibid.,* pp. 224-225.
29 *Ibid.,* p. 226.

less technical language, an equivalent of Bultmann's definition of myth as the objectivizing of non-objective reality. Here, too, is his definition of the life of faith as an authentic understanding of one's existence as a person, a genuine facing of the problem of what one ought to be.[30] Arnold's famous account of "the true meaning" of religion as *morality touched by emotion* (thus becoming righteousness — the word of religion)[31] is a Victorian version of the concept of existential involvement. His claim to have isolated the natural truth of the religious life was founded on his argument that conduct was three-fourths life. Emotion had to be added to *morality* (the word of philosophical disquisition) because where we were emotionally involved we gave the whole of ourselves, and no partial or passing thought, to the right employment of human powers.

In his sensitive study *Matthew Arnold*,[32] Lionel Trilling discusses Arnold's religious views, describing them as confused yet presenting them sympathetically. He points out that, although the moral emphasis of these views puts them in the line of Kant and Ritschl, they were also in the line of Schleiermacher.[33] The influence of Spinoza is recognized as well, especially in connection with Arnold's attempt to establish "his transcendent power in the language of naturalism."[34] (Spinoza, of course, had been one of the most potent forces acting on Schleiermacher.) We can see that at the back of Arnold's thinking, and only just failing to come forward to be recognized, there lurks a metaphysic. For instance, he made the assertion that "for science, God is simply *the stream of tendency by which all things seek to fulfil the law of their being.*"[35] Trilling notes that science canot say more than "all things act as they act," so that Arnold had no right to introduce the name of God at all, in the first place; while even more unscientific was his

---

[30] See above, p. 116.
[31] *Op. cit.*, p. 16.
[32] New York: Columbia Univ. Press, 2nd edition, 1949.
[33] *Op. cit.*, pp. 351-352.
[34] *Ibid.*, p. 340.
[35] *Literature and Dogma,* p. 31.

identification of the law of man's being with morality, in the
second. Yet Arnold seems to have meant by *science* no more
than "what is admittedly certain and verifiable" — taking
certainty and verifiability as being measured not by the standards
recognized by the physical sciences but by the standards discovered in literature. For it is through the latter that a true
estimate of "moral perception" is to be found, in his perspective.
Nothing else can justify his notion of *the stream of tendency*,
which is quite unscientific (as Trilling rightly insists) but wholly
in keeping with a Schleiermacherian understanding of the
emergence of the divine in world history. Equally with Schleiermacher, Arnold thought in terms of the progress of the human
race through the saving of the best and true self from being
overborne by the ordinary and apparent one. And, like Schleiermacher, he connected this salvation with Jesus, finding its
essence in the realm of feeling, of human self-consciousness.
But where Schleiermacher spoke of *absolute dependence,* Arnold
spoke of *righteousness.* His outlook seemed more moral than
mystical, more psychological than metaphysical. But that it
only seemed so, can hardly be doubted; for the "emotion"
which turned morality into religion was actually the recognition
of the real self, the emergence of the true spirit of man, and the
declaration of the natural truth of religion in the right employment of human powers.

A further indication that Arnold was employing an implicit
theology of immanence is to be seen in his refusal to separate
the natural and the revealed. "For that in us which is really
natural is, in truth, *revealed.* . . . If we are little concerned about
it, we say it is *natural;* if much, we say it is *revealed.*"[36] We
have here a remarkable anticipation of Tillich's definition of faith
as the state of being absolutely or unconditionally concerned.
Once again it is evident that emotion for Arnold was no mere
subjective state but a receptiveness opening the self to reality
beyond appearances (in Tillich's terminology, ecstatic reason
or the dimension of depth). It is in this context that we have

[36] *Ibid.,* p. 37.

to read his appeal to *the power not ourselves that makes for righteousness.* He argued that we had to recognize the *not ourselves* because we have not made ourselves or our nature or the world in which right conduct leads to happiness; and because, in achieving anything of worth, we must give ourselves "in grateful and devout self-surrender" to a power beyond ourselves.[37] But it is obvious that, having said so much, he could hardly refuse to say more. Logically, he should, like Schleiermacher, have gone on to speak of the Whence of our consciousness of absolute dependence, or, like Tillich, to develop an ontology based on our awareness of the power of Being. Trilling, noting the breakdown of the attempt to dismiss metaphysics and to establish a fully empirical and "scientific" religion, comments that it was his old hatred of "system" that betrayed him.[38]

So Arnold's case adds one more piece of evidence to support the contention that the empirical approach to religion is simply the metaphysical-mystical approach disguised. In attempting to produce religion without theology it shows its full dependence upon a presupposed metaphysical theology. Its earthbound God is the immanent deity discovered through the self-transcendence of the human spirit and proved by setting up a particular cosmology. Within such a context, the moral-pragmatic effort to avoid a closed system or "block universe" (as James called it) is self-defeating. No more than James's *will to believe* can Arnold's "fact of experience: *the necessity of righteousness*" shine by its own light.

A revised form of Arnold's moral interpretation of faith was advanced not very long ago by R. B. Braithwaite in his Eddington Memorial Lecture *An Empiricist's View of the Nature of Religious Belief.*[39] Braithwaite argued there that religious statements were not empirically verifiable (of course not — they expressed *Aberglaube,* Arnold would have said). But, like

[37] *Ibid.*, pp. 21-22.
[38] *Op. cit.*, p. 358.
[39] Cambridge: Cambridge University Press, 1955.

moral statements, they indicated the way in which an individual
intended to act, declaring his allegiance to certain moral principles. What was special about religious statements, however,
was that they were associated always with particular stories
which furthered the intention of the individual and strengthened
his will by adding psychological support. Even though the
stories in question were not believed to be true, they could
still serve a stimulus for action by helping to form a state of
mind. Thus, when Christians asserted that God was love or
agape they were declaring their intention to follow an agapeistic
way of life.

> To say that it is belief in the dogmas of religion which is
> the cause of the believer's intending to behave as he does
> is to put the cart before the horse: it is the intention to
> behave which constitutes what is known as religious con-
> viction.[40]

Braithwaite admitted his appreciation of Arnold's view of religion as morality tinged with emotion, and suggested that his
own view was somewhat similar.[41] But it is noteworthy that
he shows no tendency to follow Arnold into speculation concerning any power *not ourselves* which helps us to realize our
intentions in action by strengthening our wills. Rather, he takes
the more emphatically naturalistic path of Dewey by suggesting that the religious story (or myth) is sufficiently described
once it has been shown to satisfy a psychological need. Indeed,
he is careful not to suggest any reason why this need is felt
or why its satisfaction should have so decisive an effect. Consequently, he does not raise the metaphysical questions which
are posed by Dewey's theory of the power of imagination to
unify experience and thus create a universe in which ideals are
actualized. The empirical outlook has been preserved, though
at the cost of leaving us with an explanation of religion which
is somewhat *thin* (to use James's term). We are apt to wonder

40 *Op. cit.*, p. 16.
41 *Ibid.*, p. 28.

why religious faith has been such an immense force for good and evil in the history of mankind, if it is really no more than an emotional prop for moral effort. Braithwaite's presentation, moreover, seems unduly detached from the concrete situations in which believers practice their faith. It is general, rather than specific. Designed to cover all varieties of religion, it fails to be really convincing about any.

A resolute effort to remedy this latter defect in Braithwaite's teaching has been made recently in Paul M. van Buren's book *The Secular Meaning of the Gospel*.[42] Van Buren approves the "empirical attitudes" of the contemporary linguistic analysts, and he goes at least part of the way with Braithwaite, in particular.

To begin with, van Buren is determined to do without metaphysics. Standing within the Protestant tradition opposed to natural theology, he rejects the cognitive approach to faith-statements. "That approach builds its case on a natural sense of the divine, on natural religion and a natural revelation."[43] He also rejects the proposal to base Christianity on the translation of the name *God* into the *ground and end of all things* or *transcendence*. This proposed solution he terms "qualified literal theism," as contrasted with the "simple literal theism" of the Bible and of pre-scientific religious belief generally.[44] He finds Bultmann's program of demythologizing unacceptable because non-objective reality seems to him to be no more credible than the objectivized creations of myth: both are equally trans-empirical. And the same holds, of course, for any other theology claiming to have found the true meaning of the word *God*. If simple literal theism is wrong (it contradicts scientific knowledge), qualified literal theism is meaningless (it leads us off into the wilderness of metaphysics).

But, in the second place, van Buren agrees with Bultmann that the language of scripture is mythological and so unacceptable

[42] See above, p. 19 and ff.
[43] *The Secular Meaning of the Gospel,* p. 98.
[44] *Ibid.,* p. 99.

for modern man. Simple literal theism can no longer be rec-
onciled with the modern outlook, and must be done away
with. This means that it is impossible to speak meaningfully
about God. Nevertheless, religion stays. Specifically, Christianity stays. And, since it seems that we can speak meaningfully about Christianity, theology stays too. In fact, we have
here almost the reverse of the older type of empirical approach
to religion. Arnold and James, for example, thought that they
could find an empirically guaranteed God without going into
the territory of theology. Van Buren suggests that we try a
theology without God.

This apparent *tour-de-force* is achieved by pointing out
that the Christian faith has its focus in Christ, the historical
figure whose name was Jesus of Nazareth. Since that event
which is spoken of in Christian tradition as the Resurrection,
there has been a Christian Church continually in existence.
Here, then, is the empirical basis for this particular religion;
and, because we can speak meaningfully on this basis about
religious faith (what it means to "believe in" Jesus Christ),
we can proceed also to argue the principles of Christian theology. For, although the Bible and the Church Fathers and
Councils used the language of simple theism, they open to us
the empirical factors always present in the experience of the
Christian community. They tell us, in their own terms, what
Christian faith is; and, unless we attend to them, we are likely
to depart radically from the full and rich truth of Christianity.
So all we have to do is to translate the language of simple
theism into equivalent terms in the language acceptable today,
the language of the secular world (i.e., of everyone today who
does not preserve a "religious" side of himself which thinks
quite differently from his everyday self).

Translation is, we may grant, a constant requirement within
the Christian Church as the Gospel is preached in different
lands, in different cultures, and in different ages. There should
never be any reluctance to translate into one more tongue or one
more idiom "the events that have happened among us, following

the traditions handed down to us by the original eyewitnesses and servants of the Gospel" (Luke 1:1-2, New English Bible). Yet there is always the question of the adequacy of any translation. And when van Buren tells us that the language into which he proposes to translate the Gospel has no word for God or any of the other trans-empirical expressions used in previous translations, we may be excused for wondering whether this new version will be — or can hope to be — adequate. It would seem that, at the very least, our translator must make the same claim that Bultmann made so emphatically for his translation, namely, that the New Testament itself demands translation into words deliberately excluding formerly accepted notions, because the latter were no part of the original *kerygma* but belonged wholly to the language of the age. The claim to be able to translate is the claim to be able to go behind the words to the meaning of the words; and the claim to have discovered a radically new translation is the claim to have discovered a meaning obscured by previous translations. Any such claim has far-reaching dogmatic implications.

Van Buren says that his translation is required by the situation in which he finds himself as a modern man living in a secular world. Because he is a Christian, he must be one who does not live in one world when he is thinking about religion and in a totally different world during the remainder of his waking hours. This is admirably honest, but equally indicative of a dogmatic stand. Whatever *secular* means for him is henceforth declared to be the meaning of the Gospel. He has set limits which condition on *a priori* grounds the message which the traditional Christian *kerygma* may communicate to him. He may contend that his dogmatic translation contains all that really matters in Christianity (the "essence" in a new frame), but his standpoint has already decided what really matters before the translation begins.

Thus van Buren writes that "the language of faith has meaning when it is taken to refer to the Christian way of life; it is not a set of cosmological assertions."[45] The reason for the first part of this statement is that he has adopted the analytical philosophical belief (roughly that of Braithwaite) that religious faith falls into the same category as moral conviction and has to do with attitudes of mind leading to action. The reason for the second part is that he has assumed that his chosen philosophy tells us all we need to know about the cosmos, so that faith cannot (and will not be allowed to) tell us anything in this area, or even suggest that we might revise any of our presuppositions. As modern men we live in a universe adequately known through the application of the verification principle — revised so as to include statements involving the subject "I" as well as purely descriptive statements about observed phenomena. God will not fit within this universe, therefore the Gospel does not require us to think about him or about a supernatural dimension of history. It is not surprising, then, that van Buren suggests that his *Christian way of life* is a more inclusive form of Bultmann's *authentic existence*.[46] Certainly, like the latter, it supposes a prescribed cosmos into which the *kerygma* is fitted.

However, the central issue in van Buren's reformulated Christianity is the person and place of Jesus Christ. All that God meant is now summed up in this historical figure. Theology means for us Christology. In adopting this stance, van Buren believes he is in line with the most constructive trends in modern theology since the intervention of Barth on the theological scene. Jesus can be seen, on a historical view given through scriptural witness, to have been a "free man." Moreover, the *kerygma* of the early Church put the Resurrection in the first place of importance as constituting the reason for faith in him as Lord and Christ. In an empirical view this means that the freedom of Jesus "became contagious." "The Christian Gospel is the news of a free man who did not merely challenge men to become free; he set men free."[47] After the Resurrection the

45 *Ibid.,* p. 101.
46 *Ibid.*
47 *Ibid.,* p. 169.

disciples "to their joy. . .received a new perspective upon Jesus and then upon all things. . .they became free with a measure of the freedom which had been Jesus's during his life."[48]

This explanation of the meaning of the life and legacy of Jesus is very similar to the one given by Wieman. It sees a power existing in a human life, recognized by a community in touch with that life, and later spread through the community as a continuing energy. The chief difference (besides the slight one of terminology: *freedom* instead of *creativity*) is that van Buren does not go on to argue that the power which showed Jesus to be the Christ was "God" in him. He does not deduce from the phenomenon of the Christian Church that the universe is a place where freedom is always bringing about higher levels of creative good, although he does say that the empirical meaning of the confession that Jesus is the Eternal Logos is that the Christian believer sees the world as it "really" is.[49] But a vital question is raised by his self-denying ordinance of remaining silent about God. That is: what is so special about freedom? If neither the will of God nor the constitution of the universe may be invoked to support this particular value-judgment we may very well decide that contagious freedom is no concern of ours, since we are sufficiently free, for all practical purposes, without exposing ourselves to the Christian contagion. If we want extra freedom, moreover, we must strive to win it for ourselves, exactly as we must strive for all other desirable ends in life.

Van Buren's answer is that we are here on the territory called in traditional theology *faith*. He himself finds the empirical approach to faith to be best expressed in the conception of a fundamental attitude or *blik*, leading to a commitment.[50] The

[48] *Ibid.*, pp. 169f.
[49] *Ibid.*, p. 162.
[50] *Ibid.*, p. 91. The word *blik* here has been taken from R. M. Hare's defense of religious belief against Anthony Flew's arguments in *New Essays in Philosophical Theology* (London: S.C.M. Press, 1955). Van Buren expounds Hare's views and the similar views of Ian T. Ramsey (*The Secular Meaning of the Gospel*, pp. 85-91).

blik is a non-cognitive conception and it is not verifiable. It is a set of presuppositions about the world which every individual, in fact, must have; and, although it explains nothing, it gives the individual a perspective upon life and history determining all his actions. "In so far as his 'blik' is functioning, his language is the language of faith, whether he is speaking about some generally recognized religious subject, such as 'God,' or of some so-called secular subject, like politics or his job."[51] It follows that not all men will adopt the Christian *blik* — nor can the Christian argue the non-believer into believing what he himself believes. A *blik* just arises in a particular situation, as is reflected in the traditional terms: revelation, conversion, the Easter experience, and the illumination of the Holy Spirit.[52]

Now, a *blik* looks suspiciously like *Aberglaube* (more especially in its Jamesian form). In it the will to believe finds expression. And by its means van Buren, like the older thinkers who adopted the moral-pragmatic approach to religion, believes he has established an empirically rooted faith which escapes all allegiance to supernaturalism or transcendentalism. Yet the new proposals go no further than before in establishing a transcendent power in the language of naturalism. And certainly van Buren, quite as surely as Arnold or James, wishes to show that belief is no mere subjective attitude, in which every over-belief — even the most fantastic or superstitious — is both as true and as false as every other. He argues that, in the perspective of faith, the individual is conscious of his *blik* as not being selected by him but as that by which he is "grasped" and "held." "The language of faith, by referring to a *transcendent element*, indicates that something has happened to the believer, rather than that he has done something."[53]

It is a little hard to see how one can start by insisting that an empirically oriented Christianity needs neither a simple literal theism ("God") nor a qualified literal theism ("tran-

---

[51] *Ibid.*, p. 100.
[52] *Ibid.*, p. 143.
[53] *Ibid.*, p. 141. My italics.

scendence") and end up by announcing that the language of faith refers to a transcendent element. It is quite proper for a philosophical theologian, such as Tillich, to speak of being "grasped" by the power of being: he has posited from the first an ontologically guaranteed deity, Being-itself. But it is not proper for van Buren to claim that the language of faith is not a set of cosmological assertions and also to speak of being "grasped" by a particular perspective upon life and history which involves "ascribing universality to a particular man."[54] For only in a very special kind of cosmos can an individual *be* universal. We must conclude that van Buren, having bowed deity out at the front door, has smuggled it in again through the back door. He has banished the supernatural, but he has found room for the transcendental. In the name of the modern secular world-view, he has denied that Jesus Christ can be the revelation of a Heavenly Father. At the same time, he has asserted that the historical figure, Jesus of Nazareth, can be the occasion of our seeing the world as it "really" is, thus being set free. This is exactly what Arnold taught when he said that Jesus, allowing men to see "by a flash the true reason of things," revealed the power not ourselves that makes for righteousness.

Trilling remarks how, just as some people need to establish God for metaphysical completeness, Arnold needed religion to bring a sense of joy and of being fully alive.[55] So God had to be introduced indirectly: the language was naturalistic, the reference was transcendental. Pragmatists and empiricists who traffic in religion show the same motive and take the same route. James posited the will to believe because it made life worth living; and Wieman found life fulfilled in God-the-creative-Power. Van Buren, too, wishes to be assured of joy (the joy of the disciples at Easter). Consequently, he talks about contagious freedom and "convictions that life is worth living in a certain way."[56] He admits that words such as *free, love,* and *discern-*

[54] *Ibid.,* p. 140.
[55] *Op. cit.,* p. 352.
[56] *Op. cit.,* p. 194.

ment are not "empirically grounded" in the strictest sense —
which is why he uses the more general term *secular* to describe
the meaning which the Gospel has for him.[57] Yet the point is
that his explanatory language is no more empirical than Arnold's
was verifiable. He says, for example, that he uses the word
freedom instead of *faith* because the former does not lead us
"onto the slippery ground of the nonempirical."[58] Yet his preferred word is itself slippery. As linguistic philosophers have
shown, when used "positively" to mean freedom *for* something
(as he insists upon using it), it takes us from the empirical realm
to the metaphysical.[59]

To sum up, whether in the nineteenth century or the twentieth,
the moral-pragmatic approach to religious faith shows itself
to be an anti-supernaturalistic world-view which assumes an
immanent, earthbound God but does not want to admit that it
has metaphysical presuppositions. Putting the label *secular* on
such a world-view changes nothing, except perhaps to empha-
size that it is less a thinking through of the demands of faith
in the light of present knowledge than a capitulation to the
Zeitgeist. The secular meaning of the Gospel for van Buren is
essentially the same meaning admitted by Arnold and James. But,
unlike James, he has decided not to call the higher part of the
universe *God*, though continuing to think of the language of
faith as having a transcendent reference. This decision is helpful
in that it makes plain the anti-supernaturalistic attitude of the
immanentist faith — it does not in the least believe in a God
"high over all." On the other hand, the decision is a cause of
confusion in that it suggests that no divinity has been invoked
when one claims to have been grasped from outside oneself, or
that no cosmological assertions have been made when one
claims to have a right perspective on the way things are. Van
Buren's *contagious freedom* is the result of belief in the God

57 *Ibid.*, p. 195.
58 *Ibid.*, p. 123.
59 See, for example, Maurice Cranston's *Freedom, A New Analysis*
(London: Longmans, Green, 1953).

"down here" who permits our awareness of a divine quality —
call it positive freedom, creativity, joy-giving righteousness, the
New Being, or God-consciousness — transcending the empirical
(Schleiermacher's sensuous) world. And his Christocentric
theology without God is, quite as much as was Arnold's natural
Christianity, in the line of Schleiermacher. In it, too, everything
depends upon the redemption accomplished by Jesus of Nazareth.
That is to say, Jesus was the first one to exhibit how the highest
self-consciousness (freedom) can possess humanity, so that his
consciousness lives on mystically (is contagious) in the Church.
One's *blik* derives from the picture of Jesus as the Christ, the
manifestation of freedom from mere existence and for transcendence.

PART FOUR:

A Voice Affirming Heaven

10

Bonhoeffer's Religionless Christianity

PAUL VAN BUREN TELLS US THAT HIS CONSTRUCTIVE effort to present the Gospel in secular terms was inspired by Dietrich Bonhoeffer's belief that our modern world requires a "nonreligious interpretation of biblical concepts."[1] And Bishop Robinson acknowledges Bonhoeffer's plea for a non-religious understanding of God to be one of the chief influences leading him to question the traditional presentation of Christianity.[2] Since my analysis so far has led to the conclusion that the "revolutionary" proposals of Robinson and van Buren rob us of the biblical basis of the Gospel, it may be valuable now to look at what Bonhoeffer had to say about presenting Christianity to the modern, secularized world. Do his ideas also head us away from the God of scripture to an earthbound God?

There are available a number of excellent discussions of Bonhoeffer's notion of a religionless Christianity.[3] So it ought not to

[1] *The Secular Meaning of the Gospel,* pp. 1-3, 171.
[2] *Honest To God,* pp. 35-39.
[3] For example: John D. Godsey, *The Theology of Dietrich Bonhoeffer* (Philadelphia: Westminster Press, 1960); *The Place of Bonhoeffer,* edited by Martin E. Marty (New York: Association Press, 1962); Daniel Jenkins,

be necessary to belabor the point that the roots of this notion
lie in Barth's belief that religion must be set in sharp opposition
to revelation. In *Prisoner for God*[4] we read how highly he es-
timated Barth's thinking here. "He called the God of Jesus Christ
into the lists against religion, *pneuma* against *sarx*.' That was
and is his greatest service."[5] Religion as *sarx* ("flesh") stood for
every effort of man to rise to God through his own powers. In
particular, as Bonhoeffer saw it, it stood for ideas built upon
natural theology or theology of the Schleiermacherian type.
Commenting upon the apologetic theologies of Tillich and other
modern theologians, Bonhoeffer concluded:

> Barth was the first to realize the mistake that all these
> efforts (which were all unintentionally sailing in the channel
> of liberal theology) were making in having as their objec-
> tive the clearing of a space for religion in the world or
> against the world.[6]

Christian faith depended upon *pneuma* ("spirit") and was God-
given. It was not an inference from man's religious consciousness.

Being persuaded that religion was born of human speculation,
Bonhoeffer was of the opinion that Christians should not bemoan
the growing secularization of modern life and long for a return
to the so-called ages of faith. The world had "come of age."
This did not mean that men were now wise and mature in their
attitudes — far from it. Bonhoeffer, as he saw the Weimar Re-
public give way to the Third Reich, had no such illusions. It
meant that men could now understand the universe without requiring a religious underpinning for their world-view. There
was no longer any need for the concept "God" as a working

Beyond Religion; the Truth and Error in "Religionless Christianity" (London: S.C.M. Press, 1962); Gerhard Ebeling, "Dietrich Bonhoeffer" and "The
'Non-religious Interpretation of Biblical Concepts'" in *Word and Faith*.

[4] New York: Macmillan, 1957. References in this chapter are to the
edition of 1953, entitled *Letters and Papers from Prison* (London: SCM
Press).

[5] *Letters and Papers from Prison*, p. 148.

[6] *Ibid.*

hypothesis or as a *Deus ex machina,* i.e., to explain the origin of the world or to cover up the fact that we cannot explain it. If Christianity had anything vital to say to an age nurtured in science, it must not be to urge that God was still necessary as an explanation of the unknown on the "borders of human existence," where man so far had not gained control of his destiny. It must be to speak of the reality of God declared in the scriptures, the God who was truly transcendent in having to do with the whole of life, the living God. "The transcendence of theory based on perception has nothing to do with the transcendence of God. God is the 'beyond' in the midst of life."[7]

Bishop Robinson does Bonhoeffer little service by quoting this last sentence within the context of an argument stating that God is experienced in our "awareness of the transcendent, the numinous, the unconditional."[8] For that is everything Bonhoeffer does not intend, being a clear statement of the transcendence of theory. Robinson simply has assumed that Tillich's world-view is correct, and that the modern age, having rightly thrown off supernaturalism, must now learn a more sophisticated religion replacing the Old Man in the sky by the concept of ultimate reality. Actually, Tillich's theory of the God of the depths is very much what Bonhoeffer condemns when he states that God is not to be sought on the borders of existence. Tillich argues that we become aware of the depths of being in "boundary-situations" where the unconditional, the Ground of our being, cannot be overlooked — as it mostly is in our day-to-day living. Bonhoeffer's position is that a genuinely transcendent God cannot be deduced from a numinous fringe of experience making us feel that life has a transcendent meaning; for that would be to call in the religious hypothesis and to invoke the *Deus ex machina.* An abstract belief in God's attributes is "not a genuine experience of God, but a partial extension of the world."[9] But then it follows that to call our experience of the

---

[7] *Ibid.,* p. 124.
[8] *Honest To God,* pp. 52-56.
[9] *Letters and Papers from Prison,* p. 179.

depth dimension of life "God" is also a partial extension of the world and not a genuine experience of God. *Sarx* cannot claim to prove the reality of *pneuma!* Rather, this is to make room for religion, after the old liberal fashion, and to assign to God the place he must occupy in the universe. In this case, the place is at the limit of our experience. And such a place is neither truly "beyond" nor truly "in the midst of our life."

Robinson tries to equate Bonhoeffer's "beyond in the midst" with Tillich's Ground of our being "beyond naturalism and supernaturalism." He sees that both are dissatisfied with theism. But he does not see that each is dissatisfied for a completely different reason. Bonhoeffer will not rest in a speculative view of God which claims to establish *a* God, yet not necessarily the Christian God. He wants no theoretical apologetic. On the other hand, Tillich rejects theism, not because it is apologetic, but because he thinks it to be unsound, outdated apologetic. He does not believe that *any* God can be accepted by the modern mind except the God who is speculatively guaranteed to be ultimate reality. And Robinson supports Tillich's speculative idea of God because he thinks that it detaches transcendence from "the projection of supranaturalism."[10] But Bonhoeffer was of the opinion that the supernatural was no projection, but the heart of the Christian faith. His discussion of Bultmann — tantalizingly brief yet incisive — assures us on this point.

Bonhoeffer wrote of Bultmann's attempt to reduce Christianity to its essence ("the typical liberal reduction process") as a grave mistake.

> I am of the view that the full content, including the mythological concepts, must be maintained. The New Testament is not a mythological garbing of the universal truth; this mythology (resurrection and so on) is the thing itself — but the concepts must be reinterpreted in such a way as not to make religion a pre-condition of faith (cf. circumcision in St. Paul).[11]

10 *Honest To God,* p. 56.
11 *Letters and Papers from Prison,* p. 149. Cf. p. 123.

This mythology is the thing itself. In Bonhoeffer's eyes the Gospel was incurably "mythological," in the sense of piercing through the circle of human ideas and human standards about what was credible. It was a message from heaven. There could be no theological thinking without admitting the supernatural.[12]

Why then did he not stay with Barth, insisting that the Gospel is preached in the Church and must simply be accepted as given? The answer to this question is to be found in his conviction that Christians must discover a new missionary strategy in a world come of age. He disapproved of what he called Barth's "positivism of revelation." The Barthian position, although it had a true view of the substance of theology, resulted in a take-it-or-leave-it attitude where the proclamation of the Gospel was concerned. And it led to a conservative ecclesiastical reaction, to a trust-the-Church attitude contrary to the Protestant spirit. Thus the challenge of Christianity failed to reach men where they were and in a form applicable to the needs of the world of today. Bultmann had sensed the need for a truly contemporary witness, and had attempted to go beyond Barth's theological positivism. Unfortunately, he had been too eager to meet the world on its own terms. As a result, he had fallen back into the same liberalism from which Barth previously had freed us.

Bonhoeffer's own proposal was to reinterpret the full Gospel — God and miracles, biblical faith, *the thing itself* — in a "non-religious" sense. He gave hardly any indication as to how this was to be carried out. Yet he did say what he meant by interpretation in a "religious" sense. "In my view, that means to speak on the one hand metaphysically, and on the other individualistically. Neither of these is relevant to the Bible message or to the man of today."[13] So it would seem that one side of his

[12] "You cannot, as Bultmann imagines, separate God and miracles . . . Bultmann's approach is really at bottom the liberal one (i.e. abridging the Gospel) whereas I seek to think theologically" (*ibid.*, p. 125).
[13] *Ibid.*, p. 125.

program was to carry to a logical conclusion Luther's concern
for freeing the Gospel from "carnal reason." We should not allow our metaphysical presuppositions concerning the nature of
God to come between us and God's self-revelation in the Incarnation.

> The God who makes us live in this world without using
> him as a working hypothesis is the God before whom we
> are ever standing. Before God and with him we live
> without God. God allows himself to be edged out of the
> world and on to the cross. God is weak and powerless in
> the world, and that is exactly the way, the only way, in
> which he can be with us and help us. . . . This is the de-
> cisive difference between Christianity and all religions.[14]

These words remind us of Luther's warning that we should
not seek to substitute a *theologia gloriae* for a *theologia crucis,*
but should remember that to be a Christian is to see God in the
despised man Jesus.[15]

Bonhoeffer invoked Luther directly when he explained the
dangers of religious individualism. Such individualism (he
sometimes referred to it as "methodism") was not content to
stay with faith but, concentrating upon achieving a holy life,
missed the *living* of faith by trying to *win* it. Christian "worldli-
ness," on the contrary, accepted the universal human lot, and
by not aspiring to a special sanctity gained knowledge of ever-
present death and resurrection in Christ. "I believe Luther
lived a this-worldly life in this sense."[16] Moreover, religious individualism was unduly preoccupied with personal salvation.
Bonhoeffer made the startling suggestion that, if the New Testament were read in continuity with the Old, Christianity would
not be classed as a religion of salvation at all. Salvation-re-

[14] *Ibid.,* p. 164.
[15] In his essay "The 'Non-religious Interpretation of Biblical Concepts'"
Gerhard Ebeling writes that the *theologia crucis* is the key to Bonhoeffer's
thinking (*Word and Faith,* p. 158).
[16] *Letters and Papers from Prison,* p. 164. Bonhoeffer commented that
his own book *The Cost of Discipleship* was not above criticism in failing
to escape from over-concern with individual holiness.

ligions were the properly mythological ones, offering deliverance from physical death. The Old Testament, however, spoke of *historical* redemption — a living before God on earth. And, although St. Paul certainly preached the Christian hope of resurrection, he preached it in the context of sending man back to his life on earth in the service of his Lord, not in the context merely of the hope of a better world beyond the grave.

> This world must not be prematurely written off. In this the Old and New Testaments are at one. Myths of salvation arise from human experiences of the boundary situation. Christ takes hold of a man in the center of his life.[17]

In this way Bonhoeffer saw the individualistic concentration upon personal holiness and personal immortality to be a retreat from the call to discipleship. Jesus lived for others, thus proving that his was "a life based on the transcendent." Christians were called into fellowship with their Lord, not directed to a life of other-worldly piety controlled by the religious purpose of transcending the world.

If Bonhoeffer was fairly clear about the religious interpretation of Christianity to be avoided, the specific form which a non-religious interpretation of biblical concepts was to take never crystallized in his mind. He would bring up the subject only to postpone it.[18] And the "Outline for a Book" which was to expound his theme of worldly Christianity merely noted the headings to be treated: creation, fall, atonement, repentance, faith, the new life, the last things.[19] All that we can be certain about is that he had no thought of trimming the Gospel in order to accommodate it to contemporary world-views. To live in the world *etsi deus non daretur* was not to be without theological orientation. It included an understanding of what it was to live "before God" even while living "without God." The only theology to be excluded was apologetic theology.

---

17 *Ibid.*, p. 154.
18 *Ibid.*, p. 160.
19 *Ibid.*, p. 179.

The world's coming of age is then no longer an occasion
for polemics and apologetics, but it is really better understood than it understands itself, namely, on the basis of the
Gospel, and in the light of Christ.[20]

Bonhoeffer assumed that through all changes the scripture
would still bring the authentic message, and reliable theological
sign-posts (e.g., Luther) would continue to mark our road.

Thus, although we do not know how Bonhoeffer would have
developed the notion of religionless Christianity had he been
spared to bring his thought to maturity, we do know that he
could *not* have developed it by joining Tillich's "sailing in the
channel of liberal theology" in order to find God in the awareness of the transcendent, as Robinson suggests. And he could
not have developed it through van Buren's "secular" interpretation of the Gospel as a justification of his hope.[21] For van Buren's
proposals entail clearing a space for religion in the world just as
much as Tillich's do, only on the basis of a different philosophy.
The very title of his book, *The Secular Meaning of the Gospel*,
sets him totally at odds with Bonhoeffer, who repudiated the
idea of looking for meaning as a man-centered effort to find a
congenial world-view. The only meaning of the Gospel was its
real meaning;[22] and that meaning was not a system of thought
but the Man Jesus Christ. Indeed, Bonhoeffer showed the non-
Christian foundation of the Theology of Meaningfulness when
he wrote: "The word 'meaning' does occur in the Bible, but it
is only a translation of what the Bible means by 'promise.'"[23]
That was why he could dismiss Bultmann's demythologizing
program as an example of the "typical liberal reduction process."
The New Testament could not be reduced to terms expressing
the meaning that we happened to consider meaningful. Liberal-

[20] *Ibid.*, p. 149.
[21] Van Buren writes: "Our method is one which never occurred to
Bonhoeffer, but our interpretation may nonetheless serve to justify his
hope" (*The Secular Meaning of the Gospel*, p. 171).
[22] Bonhoeffer's "Outline for a Book" had for its second chapter-heading
"The Real Meaning of the Christian Faith."
[23] *Ibid.*, p. 184.

ism had failed precisely because it had "allowed the world the right to assign Christ his place in that world."[24] To find the meaning the Gospel intended was to receive the promises of God proclaimed in the Gospel, not to interpret it according to our "enlightened" tastes. Only when we had learned not to pride ourselves on our self-understanding would we find ourselves in the light of Christ. Only when we were no longer eager to make a space for religion agreeable to the *Zeitgeist* would we find that Christ had made us free on the basis of the Gospel.

Bonhoeffer compared the "religious" interpretation of the Gospel with the problem of circumcision in the early Church. St. Paul found that because Christians believed themselves to be bound to the external demands of the Law they had lost the freedom to live in the power of the Gospel. The glory of God's new deed in Jesus Christ had become obscured by the limited measure of human minds. He chided the Galatians, saying: "You started with the spiritual; do you now look to the material to make you perfect?" (Galatians 3:3, New English Bible). All this was transferred into the sphere of "religious" Christianity by Bonhoeffer, who identified religion with flesh and the revelation of God in Christ with spirit. If the "God" of natural theology, the deity who was a partial extension of the world, were to be posited as the precondition of believing the Gospel, then Christ could not be received wholeheartedly as God in human form in the midst of life, "because for Christ himself is being substituted one particular stage in the religiousness of man, i.e., a human law."[25] We can discover what the Gospel is only through accepting the promises of God and participating in the Body of Christ under its Head. To insist upon a speculative framework within which we "place" God and Christ is to bind ourselves to a human law, the product of our "carnal" imagination.

[24] *Ibid.*, p. 147.
[25] *Ibid.*

There are thorny problems which arise out of Bonhoeffer's radical dismissal of all religious conceptions as of the flesh. But his position is far from demanding the conclusions which have been proposed in the name of a non-religious interpretation of Christianity, conclusions which would reduce faith to a horizontal concern for our neighbor shorn of its vertical reference to God. For example, both Robinson and van Buren wish to make prayer a reflection upon concrete situations viewed in the light of our commitment to an outgoing life.[26] What Bonhoeffer says is that the requirement of loving God with our whole hearts does not conflict with genuine human love, but is its basis. Love of God is "a kind of *cantus firmus* to which the other melodies of life provide the counterpoint."[27] For him prayer was intimately connected with trust in the guiding hand of God upon our daily life.[28] So his wish for a "worldly" Christianity was never a denial of another world and the demand for an exclusive concentration upon this one. It was taking seriously the prayer that God's will might be done on earth as in heaven. What he deplored was not the recognition of the supernatural, but the separation of the supernatural from the natural in such a way that man was asked to choose between the secular and the Christian spheres, and was never expected to bring the two into relation. Both the Medieval Church and modern individualistic Protestantism had tried to direct the Christian into a world-disregarding holiness, contrary to the teaching of the New Testament. "And yet what is Christian is not identical with what is of the world. The natural is not identical with the supernatural or the revelational with the rational."[29] The unity of the two spheres could be realized only in Christ. That was why the New Testament proclaimed the coming of the divine reality invading and possessing the present world. That was why, too,

---

[26] *Honest To God*, Chapter 5, "Worldly Holiness," pp. 84-104; *The Secular Meaning of the Gospel*, pp. 188-90.

[27] *Letters and Papers from Prison*, p. 131.

[28] *Ibid.*, pp. 78, 177, 185.

[29] *Ethics* (London: S.C.M. Press, 1955), p. 65.

Luther protested "against a Christianity which was striving for independence and detaching itself from the reality in Christ."[30]

A supernatural God, incarnate in Christ as a supernatural reality within the world, is central to Bonhoeffer's thought. Any attempt to picture God as the reality we are prepared to call *ultimate* on the strength of our understanding of the universe can only be flesh trying vainly to turn itself into spirit, man wishing to climb to heaven. When reality actually revealed itself, it was hidden except to the eyes of faith — and still is. On the surface, it seems odd that Bonhoeffer should have written that, while most thought that Bultmann had gone too far in his demythologizing the New Testament, he himself believed that he had not gone far enough.[31] Yet he was being quite consistent. He meant what he said when he spoke of the mythology of the New Testament being *the real thing*. Bultmann "did not go far enough," because he had intended to go beyond Barth's "positivism of revelation" for the sake of speaking to a world come of age; but, in fact, he had fallen back into religious liberalism. Only his motive, which was to bring the Gospel into the world, was a step in the right direction. Unless we were prepared to go further, so Bonhoeffer believed, we were likely to fall back into an individualistic, exclusively other-worldly Protestantism promoting a reactionary ecclesiasticism.

Bonhoeffer himself did not discover how it would be possible to go further. Perhaps his vision of a consistently non-religious Christianity was an unrealistic one. Since we live in the flesh, we cannot leave behind completely the "flesh" of religion as long as we are pilgrims on the earth. We always find the treasure of the Gospel in the earthen vessels of religious concepts. But, at least, Bonhoeffer knew that to mistake the earthen vessel for the treasure was idolatry. The Gospel was for him the promises of God to be faithfully received in the Man who came down from heaven. It was because of the historic Incarnation that we

[30] *Ibid.* The whole argument is given under the title "Thinking in Terms of Two Spheres" (pp. 62-72).
[31] *Letters and Papers from Prison,* p. 125.

could know God as the beyond in the midst of our life. Religionless Christianity was his vision of faith freed entirely from
the earthbound God of human imagination. God could not be
simply that which we decided to be meaningful for us, for the
God of the Bible has said what he means by his Word, Jesus
Christ our Lord.

Conclusion

THE SCOPE OF THE PRESENT STUDY HAS BEEN BOTH wide and narrow. It has been wide in sweeping over a considerable time-span and dealing with a variety of thinkers, both classic and contemporary. But it has been narrow in keeping to a single theme, namely, the attempt to banish the supernatural in theologies purporting to reinterpret Christianity for "the modern mind." There has been no question of giving a survey of theological thought as such, or of dealing with the total outlook of any individual theologian. My concern has been to review some of the outstanding varieties of anti-supernatualism, showing how present-day theories have their roots in the past. It may be useful now to summarize with a few comments and final explanations.

The label "the Theology of Meaningfulness" was chosen as a blanket term for anti-supernaturalistic theology because it drew attention to the constant claim made by anti-supernaturalists to have found a way of making Christian faith meaningful to their generation. The point is that all such claims, by begging the question of a criterion of meaning, simply throw up a smoke-screen hiding the fact that the supernatural character of the Gospel is the vital issue. Fifty years ago, when liberal theology was a self-confident and crusading movement, it was more usual to say that Christianity must be freed from its bondage to out-worn dogmas. The newer apologetic, saying that Christian doc-trine must be stated in new images, is less candid but no less destructive in its effects.

In order to demonstrate the continuity in outlook between modern theologies of meaningfulness and the stream of liberal theology having its origin in the Enlightenment, it was necessary to look back into history. In a general survey of the pedigree of liberalism, of course, it would have been obligatory to look at other important formative influences which I have barely men-tioned: Feuerbach and Hegel, for example. However, for my present purposes, Schleiermacher is the principal witness, with Kant a rather distant second. This emphasis is dictated by the prevailing state of theological interests. Earlier in the century, Kant and Hegel would have been the chief figures to reckon with, but not now. It may seem that my analysis has over-stressed the influence of Schleiermacher today; yet there is good evidence to the contrary. Such a recent work as Richard R. Niebuhr's *Schleiermacher on Christ and Religion* is perhaps a portent. Nevertheless, it is Schleiermacher as the invisible hand laid upon the whole enterprise of making the Gospel meaningful that is still most commonly found. Almost anywhere we turn we can find apologetic which, without in the least appealing to his example, follows closely in his theological line.[1]

Naturally, this is not to say that all contemporary theologies of meaningfulness speak with a single voice. There are strong differences between them, leading often to sharp disputes. Nev-ertheless, as I have argued when writing on the subject of

---

[1] A striking recent example is Carl Michalson's *The Rationality of Faith: an Historical Critique of the Theological Reason* (New York: Scribner's Sons, 1963). Michalson speaks about faith as "historical maturi-ty," and his book is, in effect, a modern variation upon the theme of Schleiermacher's view of the world and universal history. Michalson divides *nature* from *history* as Schleiermacher divided *sensuous reality* from *self-consciousness*. His conclusions about God as the source of the world's meaning upon which we are absolutely dependent are as fully Schleier-macherian as is his thesis that faith is rational. (On the latter point cf. *The Christian Faith*, p. 67, §13 *Postscript*).

Schleiermacher's modern sons, the quarrels are essentially family quarrels. And it has been my task to insist upon the similarities and pass over (for the most part) the differences, lest the reader should fail to see the forest for the trees. Just as statesmanship is said to depend upon using large maps, so Christian clearheadedness depends upon taking a large view of theological movements. It is noteworthy, too, that there is nearly always a complete contrast in tone to be felt between theological writings taking their stand on a theory of meaning, on the one hand, and those acknowledging supernatural revelation, on the other. The whole context of the discussion in each case is so disparate, that it is surely not merely traditionalistic prejudice prompting the conviction — voiced by Bonhoeffer — that the term *theological* belongs properly to the latter alone.[2] Incidentally, it is because Bultmann wavers between the two that his thought is so equivocal. The same is true, in a rather different way, of Robinson.

To prophesy about the future or to make recommendations is no part of an enquiry, and so I have not attempted to suggest how the challenge of anti-supernaturalism is to be met. I have contented myself with bringing forward Bonhoeffer as my last witness. He proves, at least, that not every "revolutionary" theology in the twentieth century is anti-supernaturalist. And he points up the issue which is most acute for us still, namely, whether our beliefs are a response to revelation or the product of our own perspective on the universe. For the question of meaning, raised by itself, is always confused and confusing. For Christian faith the primary question is that of *authority* — of the Word that uncovers where meaning lies for us. In one of his early works Bonhoeffer put the matter succinctly: "Revelation is its own donor, without preconditions, and alone has the power to place in reality. From God to reality, not from reality to God, goes the path of theology."[3] Flesh and blood cannot bring us to the Truth that is in Christ, but only our Father in heaven.

[2] See above, p. 173 n. 12.
[3] *Act and Being* (New York: Harper & Brothers, 1961), p. 89.

Index of Subjects

187

Acknowledgments

Chapter 6 is an enlarged and revised form of an article, "Under Schleiermacher's Banner," which appeared originally in *Religion in Life,* Autumn 1963 (Copyright © 1963 by Abingdon Press), and the copyright material is here reprinted with permission. Chapter 9 incorporates my article, "Verifiable Christianity: From Arnold to Van Buren" from the *Canadian Journal of Theology,* Autumn 1965, and I am indebted for permission to reproduce the material which appeared there.

Grateful acknowledgment is also hereby made for permission to quote from the following published works:

To Abingdon Press, Nashville, Tenn., for permission to quote from *Kerygma and History,* edited by Carl E. Braaten and Roy A. Harrisville.

To Cambridge University Press, London, and to the Eddington Trustees for permission to quote from R. B. Braithwaite, "An Empiricist's View of Religious Belief"; also to the Cambridge University Press, American Branch, New York, for permission to quote from *The New English Bible: New Testament,* © The Delegates of the Oxford University Press and the Syndics of the Cambridge University Press, 1961. Reprinted by permission.

To the University of Chicago Press, Chicago, for permission to quote from Paul Tillich's *Systematic Theology*: Volume I copyright 1951 by The University of Chicago; Volume II copyright 1957 by The University of Chicago; Volume III © 1963 by The University of Chicago.

To T. & T. Clark, 38 George Street, Edinburgh, for permission to quote from Schleiermacher's *The Christian Faith,* edited by H. R. Mackintosh and J. S. Stewart.

To Columbia University Press, New York, for permission to quote from L. Trilling, *Matthew Arnold,* 2nd edition. New York, Columbia University Press, 1949.

To Doubleday & Company, Inc., New York, for permission to quote from St. Thomas Aquinas, *On the Truth of the Catholic Faith,* Volume I, translated by Anton C. Pegis.

To Farrar, Straus & Giroux, Inc., New York, for permission to quote from Karl Jaspers and Rudolf Bultmann, *Myth and Christianity*.

J. Higinbotham
Manchester
April 1978

Revolt Against Heaven

UNDER this title Professor Hamilton classes all the attacks on the supernatural in Christian revelation that have been made from the days of the Gnostics in the Early Church, and later through Schleiermacher, Bultmann, Ogden, van Buren, and Bishop Robinson with his "honest-to-God" theology, and all the fun that he poked at "the God up there" or "the God out there." Professor Hamilton shows that this is very much more serious than some of the less thoughtful readers of Bishop Robinson's book might imagine, because "Christian faith cannot simply be detached from a supernatural frame of reference." Professor Hamilton's approach is lucid, objective and thoroughly documented, and he is clearly familiar with the philosophical backgrounds and antecedents of modern anti-God theology.

Dr. Hamilton is Assistant Professor of Systematic Theology at United College, Winnipeg, Manitoba.

To Harper & Row, Publishers, Inc., New York, for permission to quote from Karl Barth, *Protestant Thought from Rousseau to Ritschl;* Dietrich Bonhoeffer, *Act and Being;* Richard B. Brandt, *The Philosophy of Schleiermacher;* Kenneth Cauthen, *The Impact of American Religious Liberalism;* Nels F. S. Ferré, *Christ and the Christian* and *Searchlights on Contemporary Theology;* D. C. Mackintosh, *Problems of Religious Knowledge;* John Macquarrie, *Twentieth-Century Religious Thought;* H. Richard Niebuhr, *Radical Monotheism and Western Culture;* Schubert M. Ogden, *Christ Without Myth;* Daniel Day Williams, *God's Grace and Man's Hope*, and *What Present-Day Theologians Are Thinking.*

To John Knox Press, Richmond, Va., for permission to quote from Karl Barth's *The Humanity of God.*

To Longmans, Green & Co. Limited, Harlow, Essex, and to The Helicon Press, Baltimore, Maryland, for permission to quote from David Knowles, *The Evolution of Medieval Thought.*

To the Macmillan Company, New York, for permission to quote from Paul M. van Buren, *The Secular Meaning of The Gospel,* © Paul M. van Buren 1963; and from Alfred North Whitehead, *Religion in the Making,* 1926.

To the Newman Press, Westminster, Maryland, for permission to quote from M. C. D'Arcy, *St. Thomas Aquinas.*

To the Oxford University Press, London, for permission to quote from Rudolf Otto's *The Idea of the Holy,* translated by John W. Harvey; and from *The Journals of Sören Kierkegaard,* edited and translated by Alexander Dru.

To Penguin Books Ltd., Harmondsworth, Middlesex, for permission to quote from Gordon Leff's *Medieval Thought*: *Augustine to Ockham.*

To Prentice-Hall, Inc., Englewood Cliffs, N. J., for permission to quote from Matthew Spinka, *Christian Thought from Erasmus to Berdyaev,* © 1962.

To Random House, Inc., New York, and to Burns & Oates Ltd., London, for permission to quote from *Basic Writings of Saint Thomas Aquinas,* Volume I, edited and annotated by Anton C. Pegis, © 1945; and to Random House, Inc., New York, for permission to quote from Etienne Gilson's *The Christian Philosophy of St. Thomas Aquinas,* translated by L. K. Shook, © 1956.

To S. C. M. Press Ltd., London, for permission to quote from Dietrich Bonhoeffer, *Letters and Papers From Prison;* J. K. S. Reid, *Our Life in Christ,* © S. C. M. Press Ltd., 1963 (published U.S.A. 1963, The Westminster Press); John A. T. Robinson, *Honest to God* © S. C. M. Press Ltd., 1963 (published U.S.A. 1963, The Westminster Press); *The Honest to God Debate,* edited by David L.

Edwards and John A. T. Robinson © S. C. M. Press Ltd., 1963 (published U.S.A. 1963, The Westminster Press). All by permission of the Westminster Press. Also for permission to quote from Michael B. Foster's *Mystery and Philosophy,* distributed in the U.S.A. by Allenson's, Naperville, Ill.

To Charles Scribner's Sons, New York, for permission to quote from Etienne Gilson, *Reason and Revelation in the Middle Ages;* D. C. Macintosh, *The Reasonableness of Christianity;* Carl Michalson, *The Rationality of Faith: An Historical Critique of the Theological Reason;* Richard R. Niebuhr, *Schleiermacher on Christ and Religion*: *A New Introduction;* Henry P. Van Dusen, *The Vindication of Liberal Theology*: *A Tract for the Times.*

To the Westminster Press, Penn., for permission to quote from Richard Kroner, *Speculation and Revelation in the Age of Christian Philosophy,* © W. L. Jenkins, 1959. Published by the Westminster Press. And for permission to quote from *Agape and Eros* by Anders Nygren, translated by Philip S. Watson. Published U.S.A., The Westminster Press, 1953, and also by permission of S.P.C.K., London.

To the World Publishing Company, New York, for permission to quote from *Existence and Faith; Shorter Writings of Rudolf Bultmann,* selected, translated and introduced by Schubert M. Ogden, Copyright © 1960 by Meridian Books, Inc.; *A Handbook of Christian Theology,* edited by Marvin Halverson and Arthur H. Cohen, Copyright © 1958 by Meridian Books, Inc.

To the Yale University Press, New Haven, for permission to quote from John Dewey, *A Common Faith,* copyright 1934.